SANDRA
SCHMIRLER

SANDRA SCHMIRLER

The Queen of Curling

PERRY LEFKO

Published in 2001 by
Stoddart Publishing Co. Limited
895 Don Mills Road, 400-2 Park Centre, Toronto, Canada M3C 1W3
PMB 128, 4500 Witmer Estates, Niagara Falls, New York 14305-1386

First published in hardcover in 2000

www.stoddartpub.com

To order Stoddart books please contact General Distribution Services
In Canada Tel. (416) 213-1919   Fax (416) 213-1917
Email cservice@genpub.com
In the United States Toll-free tel. 1-800-805-1083 Toll-free fax 1-800-481-6207
Email gdsinc@genpub.com

10 9 8 7 6 5 4 3 2

National Library of Canada Cataloguing in Publication Data

Lefko, Perry
Sandra Schmirler: the queen of curling
Includes index.
ISBN 0-7737-3275-6 (bound). — ISBN 0-7737-6275-2 (pbk).
1. Schmirler, Sandra. 2. Curling — Canada — Biography. I. Title.
GV845.62.S36L43 2000   796.964'092   C00-932148-9

Cover Design: Bill Douglas @ The Bang
Text Design: Tannice Goddard

THE CANADA COUNCIL | LE CONSEIL DES ARTS
FOR THE ARTS | DU CANADA
SINCE 1957 | DEPUIS 1957

*We acknowledge for their financial support of our
publishing program the Canada Council, the Ontario Arts
Council, and the Government of Canada through the
Book Publishing Industry Development Program (BPIDP).*

Printed and bound in Canada

To Norm Casola, the heart of the Toronto Argonauts in their back-to-back Grey Cup championship seasons in 1996–97. May people such as Normie, Sandra, and my sister Robyn live forever in our hearts and may the day come when a cure for cancer is discovered.

Contents

SANDRA
SCHMIRLER

Prologue

I feel privileged to have been allowed to write the life story of Sandra Schmirler with the authorization and cooperation of her husband, Shannon England, and her mother, Shirley. I am indebted to both for so much. Besides being a great source of knowledge, they were an inspiration, providing me with intimate details during an emotionally difficult time in their lives. During the research and writing of the book, the source of Sandra's strength and constitution became apparent to me.

I respected Sandra as a curler and even more as a person. She impressed me more than any other athlete I've encountered because of her joy and her spirit and her appreciation for what mattered most in life.

I visited Sandra five days before she left for Moncton, New Brunswick, in February 2000, to work on the broadcast of the Canadian national junior championships and to tell the country about her cancer struggle. I had two reasons for wanting to see her: to interview her for a newspaper article and to ask if I could write a book about her life.

"Do you think anybody would care?" she wondered. For all she had accomplished, growing up in grassroots Saskatchewan and becoming the greatest skip in the history of women's curling, Sandra never saw herself the way others did. Winning three Canadian and world titles and the first Olympic gold medal in women's curling did not make Sandra feel like the queen of the curling world. She remained humble, unaffected by her worldly accomplishments.

I will forever cherish the opportunity I had to visit Sandra before she left for Moncton. She greeted me at the door wearing a black poor-boy cap that, coupled with her glasses, seemed to frame her face so perfectly, so naturally. She had lost weight, but joked that she could now fit into skinny clothes. And when I commented on her voice, which had become raspy because of her radiation treatments, she cracked that she'd probably have to retire her trademark squeaky curling voice.

I will also cherish the opportunity I had to attend her funeral with some special people, some of whom I really did not know well beforehand. I happened to be in Saskatoon for the Brier two days after Sandra died, but as a journalist and someone who would likely be writing a book about her, I felt the need to attend her memorial service, which was really a celebration of life. I caught a ride from Gerald Shymko, who skipped Saskatchewan's entry in the 1999 Brier. Gerald earned the nickname the Jolly Grain Giant in the tournament because he is a big man who farms for a living. Gerald also "chauffered" Paul Wiecek of the *Winnipeg Free Press*, Bruce Deachman of the *Ottawa Citizen*, and Prince Edward Island curlers Kim Dolan and Rebecca Jean MacPhee.

We crammed into Gerald's 18-year-old Olds 98 — complete with duct tape on the driver's-side door and an odometer that had been turned back a few times — and departed for the three-hour journey to Regina just after 7 a.m. The funeral was to take place six hours later, but we wanted to arrive early to secure seats. We bonded during our trip, exchanging stories, about both Sandra and ourselves, which helped speed the time and ease the cramped quarters. I was squeezed in between Gerald and Paul, who could pass for a small forward in basketball.

Upon entering the city, we passed a Husky gas station that had a massive Canadian flag, which I'm told measures 60 feet by 40 feet and is the largest in the province. In honour of Sandra, it had been lowered to half mast, as had many provincial and Canadian flags, but this one stood out. As it flapped strongly in the early-morning prairie breeze, it symbolized to me the spirit of Sandra, a larger-than-life Canadian figure.

On the drive back to Saskatoon, Gerald did a radio interview and summed up what Sandra meant to Canadian curling, and to Saskatchewan in particular.

"England had Lady Di. Sandra was our Queen."

They were both known as the Queen of Hearts. In Sandra's case it referred to the heart-shaped crests she collected each time she won a provincial title. And similar to Diana, Sandra died at age 36 and left behind two children she adored.

I hope when Sandra's two children, Sara and Jenna, are older this book will help them understand more about their mother and what she accomplished in life, both as an athlete and, more importantly, as a person.

"We have two precious little girls and hopefully we'll instill in them the values that somehow we did with Momma," Shirley Schmirler told me. "I don't know how we did that. I don't know how we raised that champion. It just happened."

For that we can all be thankful, even if we couldn't have her forever. Instead, we will have her in our thoughts and our hearts.

. . . . . .

I had hoped Sandra would survive cancer and become a spokesperson and inspiration for others battling the disease. Unfortunately, the woman who seemed capable of winning everything could not defeat a disease that her doctors could not completely identify.

"I thought she represented the best of Canadiana," longtime friend and team associate Pat Reid said. "She was just a warm, clean-cut, vibrant young woman who had a passion for a sport and turned that into three world championships and an Olympic gold medal, all the while being the girl next door — someone who loved her kids and loved being a wife and a mother and worked part time. She could have been anybody, in that sense."

"But This Is Biggar"

The story of the girl who grew up to become the queen of the curling world began in Saskatchewan, Canada, specifically in a small town ironically named Biggar. It was just another square mile of prairie when the first pioneers came to the district around 1907, principally working in farming and the railway. In the summer of 1908 Biggar received its name from William Hodgins Biggar, the solicitor of the Grand Trunk Pacific Railway, which was the forerunner of the Canadian National Railway. The railway's board of directors took turns naming the divisional points — where the railroaders lived —

after themselves or their birthplaces in Scotland. Biggar evolved from a hamlet to a village to official town status in 1911.

And, it didn't take long for Biggar to acquire a slogan that would one day become famous. Legend has it that in 1914, the first survey crew that came to Biggar decided to have some fun after attending a Halloween dance. The "spirited" crew painted the town sign, "New York Is Big. But This Is Biggar." The first official sign was put up in June 1954, but it took the town's most famous sporting hero to put Biggar on the map by winning a gold medal in curling in the 1998 Winter Olympics.

Sandra's parents, Art and Shirley, moved to Biggar in 1959, a year after marrying in Saskatoon, an hour east of the town. Art worked as a telegraph operator for CN. Shirley had worked as a hospital nurse's aid, but gave up her career to become a full-time mother. They had three children, all girls, starting with Carol on December 15, 1959, Beverley on January 12, 1961, and Sandra on June 11, 1963. Sandra was born with a club foot and had to have a cast on it for the first two months, but that obviously didn't slow her procession to athletic greatness.

Sandra displayed a feisty spirit at the age of one, refusing to sleep in her crib, which prompted some early battles of wills with her mother. She also had a lovely smile, a feature that became her trademark. In an autobiographical picture book she made for a Grade 5 class project, Sandra made reference to the smile she already possessed as a four-month-old.

"There were many more smiles before this one but this is one of the biggest smiles I ever gave, and you must admit for four months it's pretty big."

She also developed her quick wit at a young age, as evidenced by another caption under a drawing of her in her infancy. "I tried very hard to color like an artist but somehow it didn't work. I always went off the lines but at fourteen months, I guess, you're not supposed to be another Lonardo Devinchy!"

In 1964 Art and Shirley completed their fourth and final move in Biggar. They bought a 1,282-foot house built before 1930, and it has become somewhat of a landmark. More than 30 years after they moved into their house and well past the time their daughters had moved out, Art and Shirley watched suspiciously from the window as a man snapped a picture of their home one day. It turned out he simply wanted a picture of the home where the famous "Schmirler the Curler" was raised. In many ways, it was not unlike someone snapping a photo of the home where the Great Gretzky or Air Jordan grew up.

For the first couple years in their new home, the sisters slept in a room on the main floor next to their parents, who tried to keep the surroundings similar to the previous home. When the children were emotionally ready, they were moved to a room upstairs. Carol and Sandra occupied one end of the room, while Beverley had the other end. Many times in the early part of the winter, Carol had Sandra snuggle in with her at night because her youngest sister was like a firebox.

"Her body had a lot of heat coming off it," Carol recalled.

Although the siblings became extremely close in their 30s, especially in the final months of Sandra's life, they didn't exactly have a fondness for one another in childhood.

"I really didn't want to be seen with my younger sister," Carol said. "Sandra and Beverley pretty much disliked me — a lot. We didn't get on well until after the first year I left home after high school."

"Carol and Sandra *never* got along," Beverley added.

On one occasion, Sandra stole her sisters' Easter chocolates wrapped in decorative tin cups. Fingers were pointed squarely at Sandra, but she swore she didn't do it. However, that was after she asked her parents if the person who confessed to stealing the sweets would be grounded and they responded "probably."

While Sandra liked playing with dolls, she also had an affinity for pets. And the Schmirler family had lots of them, including a cat, Princess, a dog, Cookie, and a bird, Cherper, which Sandra brought home one day.

"I found him sitting on the sidewalk so I ran after him," she said in her autobiographical class project. "I thought it would fly away but it hopped away. It couldn't fly, so I caught it. I took it home and we kept it (in a birdcage) through the summer until it knew how to fly, how to catch worms and eat them."

One of the few blips in Sandra's happy childhood happened in Grade 3. In fact, in her project she calls it her worst day in school, but it clearly illustrates her leadership at a young age. She befriended a girl named Corinne, who sat next to her in class. On this momentous day, the two girls were bothered by two boys, Tim Newton and Donnie Phillips. They took Corinne's book, which the two girls tried frantically to retrieve. Sandra figured if she took something belonging to the boys they would return Corinne's book, so she grabbed Tim Newton's ruler. He asked for it back but Sandra said she would only give it up if he gave Corinne's book back to her. Tim grabbed the ruler but Sandra refused to let go and it snapped.

"The thought went through my mind, 'THE STRAP! THE STRAP!' I almost died. Tim was yelling at me and I was defending myself, then *ring*, the incoming bell rang. The teacher, Miss Kaluzy, was mad and I had to give Jim 10 cents to buy a new ruler. Thank goodness I didn't get the strap.

"A few days later I asked Miss Kaluzy if I could go get a drink. While I was out there getting a drink, Tim Newton came out and said I didn't have to pay 10 cents for the ruler. Boy, what a relief!"

It was around that age that Sandra chipped her two front teeth in an accident while riding around on a plastic duck in a friend's basement. It was not until the age of 30, after she received some money for during a commercial following her first world championship, that Sandra could afford to fix her teeth — and cap her championship smile.

Sandra's photo autobiography included her first picture, a snapshot of her puppy sitting comfortably on a cushion. This is the final photo in the assignment, and the caption shows what made this woman so special.

"The first picture I ever took was of our puppy. What a cute picture! I had a pretty good life and I hope I'll have a better one in the future." She also wrote, "Last Christmas, Mom and Dad thought the family was lonesome, so they told Santa to bring a dog, so Shirley and Art's family is complete and always will be."

Not surprisingly, Sandra received a grade of excellent on her assignment.

Besides her love for animals, Sandra had a passion for sports. She liked swimming, in particular speed swimming, and competed regularly in tournaments as a member of the Biggar Barracudas. By the time she completed high school, Sandra had won numerous provincial medals in speed swimming. She also liked to play softball and slo-pitch, but although Sandra could hit and field with aplomb, she lacked running skills.

Sandra's eldest sister, Carol, recalled her youngest sibling taking a lot of abuse and teasing in school from kids at about Grade 7. While Sandra had some close friends, she also had her detractors.

"They were just snots," Carol said. "Every class has two or three girls whom they pick on. Sandra had more close friends who were boys."

The Schmirlers had a rule that prevented their daughters from fighting, but one day Shirley made an exception. She phoned the school and told the administrators that if Sandra hit a particular girl who was taunting her, she had permission from her mother. After being constantly jabbed with a pin by this girl, Sandra literally took matters into her own hands in the school yard and punched her pesky enemy. Or, as Carol put it, she "nailed" her.

In Grade 7, her first year of junior high school, Sandra began curling, which was offered as part of the physical education program.

Similar to many Saskatchewan towns, Biggar had curling as

part of its social and recreational culture. Curling originated in Scotland in the 1500s, but came to Canada in the 1700s, eventually becoming a staple of the Canadian prairies, particularly Saskatchewan because of a huge influx of Scottish settlers. The people played the sport socially and, in some cases, engaged in friendly competitions with nearby towns. Curling has been part of Biggar's makeup since the building of the first club in 1914. There have been different clubs over the years, including the current one where Sandra began her journey to become the queen of curling.

You might say Sandra was born to be a curler. Both of her parents played the sport, having been exposed to it through *their* parents. Sandra's maternal grandfather, Adolph MacLeod, played on a prosthetic leg after becoming disabled fighting for Canada in World War I. His wife, Mabel, regularly played the competitive bonspiel circuit and, according to Shirley, she likely would have been a quality club player in this era.

The MacLeods curled in a small town with two sheets of natural ice. Sometimes the games' scheduled starting times were delayed until the ice could freeze properly, which extended the matches into the early-morning hours. But, the MacLeods loved to curl and often replayed the game the following morning on the kitchen table with salt and pepper shakers.

Although it has changed over the course of time, the game Sandra learned as a child is still relatively the same today. Each team has four players who follow one another in a rotation, beginning with the lead, followed by the second, third, and skip. The teams take alternate turns throwing 42-pound rocks shaped out of granite towards a group of rings called the house. Each player throws two rocks per end. The rings measure 12 feet, 8 feet, 4 feet, and one foot in width, the last of which is called the button. Points are awarded to the team with the rock (or rocks) closest to the button at the conclusion of each of the 10 ends (although a game can finish sooner if one team surrenders). There could be a variety of hits and rolls by the time the final shot is delivered because each team has a chance to move its own rocks and the opposition's. Teams can influence their individual rocks by sweeping the path in front of them to maintain a straight path or line and go farther.

In many ways, the curling sheet is like a golf green and the object is to try to determine the runs or bends closest to the final resting place. Some neophytes describe curling as shuffleboard on ice, but to the people who play it with zeal, determination, and desire, it is more like a game of chess in which you try to outsmart your opponent with strategy that involves setting up a key move well ahead. It takes years of practice to master the game, which Sandra clearly did.

Were it not for a critical decision she made at a young age, Sandra might never have curled at all, or at least played the game with such passion. In an effort to try to expose kids to different athletic programs, the school's principal decreed that students could participate in only one sport per season. Sandra had to choose between curling and basketball, a choice that caused her such great consternation that she called her mother, who by that time had gone back to work as a nurse's aid. Shirley asked if the decision could wait until she came home following her shift, at which time Sandra chose curling.

Beverley said the decision really didn't break Sandra's heart because basketball included running, which Sandra clearly didn't enjoy. However, Shirley found it surprising that Sandra liked curling, because it moved considerably slower than volleyball and badminton, two sports in which her youngest daughter excelled and won provincial medals.

From Grades 7 to 9, Sandra received coaching from Bob Anderson, the vice-principal of Biggar High School. She played third on a team skipped by Anita Barber (now Silvernagle), whom Sandra had known since Grade 5. Karen Sapsford played lead and Connie Ries threw second stones.

"Sandra threw a great rock even way back then," Anita said.

Even though Anita lived 20 miles away from Biggar and was bused to school, she and Sandra became close friends and occasionally slept at each other's homes. Sometimes the two played on teams with Anita's parents in mixed bonspiels, which was not unusual for tournaments in small towns without an abundance of players.

Around the time they were in Grade 9, Sandra and Anita wanted to improve their skills and play with older women in the ladies' league, so they hooked up with Shirley and her friend. Shirley had resumed curling a few years earlier after a long absence because of work and family commitments.

"These two girls put 'em in the house, all we had to do was guard 'em up and we won the trophy that year," Shirley recalled. "Later on, when Sandra was in Grade 11 or 12, I remember her coming to a bonspiel with me in nearby Perdue. She was amazing as a third. We lost one game and people didn't know how that happened. We just curled incredibly. When you've got a third as good as Sandra was back then — she just did everything that she wanted — it's quite easy as a skip."

But, success had its price. The two youngsters, especially Sandra, had too much competitive drive.

"She wasn't necessarily fun to curl with," Shirley recalled laughingly. "I was not her calibre, even back then. I was new at skipping — in a small town you kind of get pushed into it."

Sandra's sister Carol concurred. "It wasn't fun doing anything competitive with Sandra. She could be tough. She just wanted to win all the time, it didn't matter what she was doing."

Mel Tryhuba, Sandra's coach in high school from Grades 10 to 12, had a different assessment of Sandra's contentious competitive drive.

"She wanted to do exceptionally well, do her best," he said. "She didn't mind losing as long as she knew she did her best."

"She wasn't a tyrant or anything, but she hated to lose," Anita recalled. "She loved to win. Everybody does, but she was more passionate about it. If we lost she would not be mad at us, just disappointed, I guess, especially if she knew we were a better team. She was just very competitive. She didn't like to lose, so she just made sure she didn't do that.

"If you look at the history of her world championship team, they suffered lots of losses. When you think back, you think they had a lot of glory — and they did — but they suffered a lot of losses along the way. Every loss you have you learn from it, and she would find something in it that she could learn what not to do next time. She was a very smart skip."

The high-school team changed slightly when Connie Ries moved and Sharlee Heather inherited her spot. The foursome had local success but came up short at the Grades 10 and 11 district level, losing both times. One loss meant instant elimination so there was little room for error.

In Grade 12, the foursome did not lose en route to the provincial championship, which it won handily. The team's success ended there because the national high-school competition had been dropped five or six years earlier.

Shirley never anticipated her daughter's interest in curling would lead to anything more than just enjoying the game, but Mel noted a difference in Sandra from other players. His prized pupil's thirst for knowledge made her stand out from Biggar's other stellar group of athletes. She yearned to understand why things were done in a certain way, such as placing the hand in a certain position when throwing a curling stone. She listened to the coaches and applied what they taught her. The more she learned, the more she wanted to learn, a trait she carried into adulthood. Whether it was her provincial women's team coach, Anita Ford, or national coach, Lindsay Sparkes, Sandra always sought advice to improve her game.

· · · · · ·

In the fall of 1981, Sandra enrolled in computer science at the University of Saskatchewan in Saskatoon, but did not have much success in her first year and switched to physical education in her second. Her sister Beverley was enrolled in education at the university at the same time but did not see much of Sandra, who continued her curling education.

"I was never really a curling fan," Beverley confessed. "I thought curling was the most ridiculous game there ever was. I don't any more."

Sandra earned a place on one of the university women's two curling teams. In her second season, she hooked up with Laurie Secord (now Humble), who had played on another team the first season. Laurie grew up in Eston, a small town southwest of Biggar, and knew Sandra, having competed against her at the district sports level.

"Sandra kind of stuck out because she had this wonderful delivery — even back then she got so low — and was an excellent shotmaker," Laurie said. "She was someone you were going to try and link up with."

The two women were only a month apart in age and their friendship thrived playing university curling. They had similar interests and often double-dated because their boyfriends were good friends. The dating didn't develop into anything serious, but Sandra and Laurie's curling futures definitely did. They were about to hit the big time for the first time in their curling careers.

In the spring of their second school year, Sandra and Laurie hooked up with Carol Davis and Heather MacMillan, both of whom were about seven years older. Carol Davis, a veteran of the Saskatoon women's circuit, was looking to form a new team the following season and became aware of Sandra's talents through the curling grapevine. She contacted Sandra to see if she wanted to play in a weekend cashspiel (a competition for money) in Regina. Carol told Sandra she didn't have anybody else lined up, but that didn't deter the university students from teaming together. Carol convinced another veteran, Heather MacMillan, who had played only briefly that year, to join the two for the spiel. When Carol asked Sandra if she knew anybody who could fill out the foursome, she recommended Laurie. The team was complete.

Carol and Sandra drove in one car and Heather and Laurie, who had never met, drove in another for the three-hour trip to the Caledonian Club, site of the spiel in Regina. It was a chance to make history and money.

"We introduced ourselves, jumped in the cars, and drove to Regina," Carol Davis said. "I was 28 or 29 at the time and to them I was middle-aged. Laurie still calls me Mom."

The foursome won the spiel, pocketing some $5,000. Although this was a large amount of money at the time, the success did not surprise the four. They meshed quickly and stayed together the following season, winning regularly on the cash circuit while sharing fun times off the ice.

"It seemed like everything just fit — we just really enjoyed one another," Carol said.

The foursome qualified for the provincial playdowns, but lost in the final to Saskatoon's Lori McGeary. She advanced to the national tournament, the Scott Tournament of Hearts, which brings together one representative from each of the provinces' playdowns, one representative from the Territories, and the reigning champion.

Carol Davis said that because Sandra and Laurie were young, they might not have appreciated how difficult it would be to reach that level again despite the quality of the team. Carol had learned the lesson already. She had won the provincial high school curling championship in her first year and three years later won the Canadian junior championship, but discovered it's not always easy to stay on top.

Laurie acknowledged she and Sandra were pretty naive then and had a lot to learn about the game and about winning and losing.

"We thought we were pretty hot stuff and we took that loss really hard," Laurie said. "On the other hand, we knew we were young and would have other opportunities. We never, ever took losing really well. We were sore losers. We'd pout a lot. After [losing] the provincial final, we won the all-star awards and we couldn't even smile or say thank you. You learn as you go along."

Sandra and Laurie displayed their youth in other ways, too. They were in awe of high-profile curlers. Laurie recalled being at a function for the Super League — the organized weekly round-robin competition for elite local teams. The event attracted national and world champion Rick Folk from Saskatoon and teammates Ron Mills and Jimmy and Tommy Wilson.

"Sandra said, 'Oh, my God, I'm sitting beside a world champion,'" Laurie said.

Laurie recalled another humorous incident that illustrates the innocence of the twenty-somethings. It happened in a game at the Nutana Club in Saskatoon against 1984 Canadian and world champion Connie Laliberte of Manitoba.

"We were just poopin' our drawers because we were playing a world champion," Laurie remembered. "We idolized those teams because they were everything we wanted to be. I always thought of that as the years went on. Sandra idolized these people and then went on to so many bigger and better things than many women's teams."

Sandra's ability did not go unnoticed. Ontario skip Marilyn Bodogh, who became the Canadian and world champion in 1986 when she was known as Marilyn Darte, watched Sandra with amazement while at the Nutana Club.

"I knew instantly she had what it took," Marilyn said. "You could just tell. I remember saying to myself, 'God, she's into this game. Look at her. She's all over the ice. She's scratching. She's clawing. She looks like me out there.' She wanted it so bad."

Carol Davis's team did not enjoy the same dream season in its second and, ultimately, its last year. While the team had some success on the cash circuit, it failed to do much in the provincial playdowns. Sandra graduated with a Bachelor of Science in Physical Education in the spring of 1985 and moved to Regina, looking for employment and to extend her curling career.

Carol Davis played for one more season and then headed to Calgary. She still wonders to this day what might have been had she, Heather, Sandra, and Laurie taken their first-year success one step higher in the second year.

"Sandra went on to absolute greatness and [the other team-mates] kind of muddled in obscurity," Carol said. "That [second year] was a real turning point. We always thought, 'If we had won, what roads would our lives have taken?'"

"Schmirler the Curler"

W hen Sandra prepared to move to Regina in 1985 after graduation, word quickly spread throughout the local curling community. Kathy Fahlman, who had won the Canadian mixed championship in 1984 playing third for Randy Woytowich, needed a third for her team and called Sandra asking her to join her team from the Tartan Club. Sandra was already recognized in Saskatchewan as a talented player and Kathy had seen that talent first-hand playing against her.

A couple of weeks after the initial conversation, Sandra agreed to join Kathy's team, which also included second Jan

Betker, who also played on Randy Woytowich's 1984 championship team, and lead Sheila Schneider.

Sandra found employment as a swimming lesson instructor and lifeguard at the North West Leisure Centre, a position for which she was over-qualified but content nevertheless. It was here she received the nickname Schmirler the Curler, although it didn't really come into regular play until 12 years later. Her supervisor, Bev Kozar, gave her the nickname to distinguish her from the other employees.

"I have so many staff, and because I don't do the direct hiring, if I want to remember an individual, I'll make mental notes about how to do that," Bev explained. "Schmirler the Curler clicked for me in my mind and also because of the small-town connection that she and I shared. That was the way I remembered her and kept track of where she was and what she was doing.

"[The nickname] was a joke. Nothing bothered Sandra. She looked at the positive of everything. I wouldn't have mentioned it to her if I thought she would be offended. I knew that she would say, 'That's a good way of thinking.'"

The competitive streak friends and family had seen in Sandra growing up started to become apparent to her new teammates. On one occasion after a loss, Sandra stormed out of the Caledonian Club, forgoing the normal practice of having a social drink after the game. Kathy addressed the issue by sitting down with Sandra and discussing her attitude.

"We'd always go upstairs and have a beer or whatever and

I remember wondering where she was and somebody said she just left," Kathy recalled.

The discussion with Kathy helped Sandra to control her fiery temper, and she started to mature as a curler and a person.

The squad had marginal success the first season, but really took off in year two, doing well on the cashspiel circuit and qualifying for the 1987 provincial championship in Yorkton. They made it to the final, but collectively suffered a serious case of nervousness. Kathy huddled with the team in the fifth-end break and pumped her players up.

And they found a way to win, earning a trip to Lethbridge, Alberta, for the Scott Tournament of Hearts, sponsored by Scott Paper Limited. Sandra's success caused quite a stir at the North West Leisure Centre, which suddenly had a celebrity on its staff. In a curling-rabid province such as Saskatchewan, making it to the national championship made Sandra an instant star.

"It was with a little disbelief that we discovered we had some-body who's a good swimmer and lifeguard and instructor and who was also so good in a totally different sport," Bev Kozar said. "She was the first person who did anything on a major scale among the staff."

Sandra had her own support staff for the tournament: her parents, sister Carol and her husband Mike, and Sandra's mater-nal grandmother. Beverley couldn't be there.

"It was a big party," Carol recalled. "It was so exciting. I'd never been to an event like that before and neither had the rest of our family. It was so much fun. Grandma was right into it.

She'd sit up in the stands and crochet her heart out."

Meanwhile, back in Regina at the North West Leisure Centre, Sandra's fellow employees watched the Scott on television and listened to the radio reports. The tournament is played over two weekends, beginning with a round-robin and then moving into the semi-finals and final playoffs.

While each of her teammates played exceptionally well and earned all-star awards, Kathy struggled badly. The team finished tied for third after the round-robin but lost the tiebreaker to Quebec. The experience still bothers Kathy.

"For some reason I just mentally crashed and burned in Lethbridge," Kathy lamented. "Up until that point I had taken the leadership role, and I wasn't able to do that in Lethbridge. I know Sheila and Jan and Sandra realized I was struggling but not once did we get together as a team and say, 'What's wrong here?'

"We were quite young. I think I was 26. I just didn't know enough to get together with the team and say, 'I'm scared to death out here. My knees are knocking and I don't know what to do.' We just went out there and tried to do our best but I couldn't shake it."

Nonetheless, it was a learning experience and something for the team to try to avoid the following season if they made it back to the Scott.

• • • • • •

While Sandra's curling career started taking off in Regina, she also developed a love interest that eventually led to marriage.

Bev Kozar and another colleague, Leanne Winter, decided to play the role of matchmaker and fix Sandra up with Del Peterson, the program specialist where Sandra worked. Sandra and Del were still both relatively new employees there.

"Sandra was just the most likable, pretty person you'd ever want to meet, so it was like 'Oh, well, she's got to be for Del,'" Bev Kozar said.

"She really fell in love with Del's family — his parents were incredible to her," Sandra's sister Carol recalled.

Sandra and Del married August 1, 1987, at the Anglican Church in Biggar. Sandra's bridesmaids included her two sisters and Jan Betker. The reception was held at the new town hall, where a crowd of almost 200 joined the happy couple. The newlyweds, who had even taken dancing lessons in preparation for their wedding, celebrated their first dance with a song by the Electric Light Orchestra.

When the curling season renewed in the fall, the Fahlman team earned a selection to the Olympic Trials in Calgary. The Trials involved eight men's and eight women's teams playing in separate round-robin tournaments. The winner of each division earned a ticket to represent Canada in the 1988 Winter Olympics, in which curling would be a demonstration sport for the first time in some 60 years. The Fahlman foursome barely received a passing glance in the women's competition won by Vancouver's Linda Moore.

The Fahlman team came up one game short in the 1988 provincial playdowns, losing the final to Michelle Schneider's team from Regina. Before the 1988–89 season, lead Sheila

Schneider left the Fahlman team and was replaced originally by Cathy Trowell. Cathy was pregnant at the time and could play only half the year, handing off her duties to her sister, Joan Inglis. In this, its last season together, the Fahlman foursome failed to qualify for the provincials.

Kathy had lost confidence as a skip and decided to accept an offer to play vice-skip for Michelle Schneider, thus removing the pressure on herself to have to make the clutch final shots.

"I thought long and hard about my decision and for me it was something I had to do," Kathy said.

Sandra and Jan recruited two other players, Susan Lang to play skip and Gertie Pick to play lead, but the new foursome did little of any consequence in the 1989–90 season. Kathy Fahlman, meanwhile, made it back to the Scott that season with Michelle Schneider.

After the one season with Susan Lang, Sandra and Jan decided to form a new team. Jan hadn't skipped since high school, and Sandra barely had any experience at the position but figured she could do it. Now they had to find some players willing to join them. They recruited Joan Inglis, who had played briefly with them two years before, to play second. Joan had curled with her sister, Cathy, the following year. But Cathy had become pregnant again, which left Joan available to join another team.

It turned out to be a great move for Joan — and not just for curling reasons. Sandra fixed Joan up with her future husband, Brian McCusker, on a mixed curling team that won the 1992 Saskatchewan provincials.

Meanwhile, Sandra's team enlisted its final member when

Joan recommended Marcia Gudereit, a teammate from the previous year. Although Marcia lacked competitive experience, playing principally at the club level, she teamed well with Joan. They would form the front end, with Marcia at lead and Joan playing second, followed by Jan at third and Sandra skipping.

Team Peterson — Sandra used her married name at the time — had been formed for the 1990–91 curling season. Because the skip is essentially the captain of the team, Sandra had to learn to control her temper or lose her fellow players' support. Shirley Schmirler believes Marcia's inexperience taught Sandra to be more understanding.

The Peterson foursome clicked in its first season, winning the provincial championship and earning a ticket to the Scott, the second one for Sandra and Jan but the first for Marcia and Joan. The fact that Sandra advanced so far in her first season skipping did not surprise Brian McCusker.

"Everyone [in the Saskatchewan curling community] had the opinion that Sandra was a really good player, but thought she would not be good as a skip because nobody had seen her skip before," Brian said. "That's the way people think in curling. People think there are skips and there are others who can't skip no matter how good they are. My opinion was that she was the best women's curler in Canada — she was the best shooter, made the most shots. I had skipped her a little in a mixed bonspiel the year before and she was consistent on the broom [target]. Just watching her and how many shots she made in games, I figured she'd probably be pretty good, but you never knew. Some players just aren't good when they play skip."

The 1991 Scott took place in Saskatoon, and once again the Schmirler clan came to support Sandra and her team. Along with Art and Shirley, the contingent included Sandra's sister Carol and her husband Mike, Grandma MacLeod, and a large gathering from Biggar. One notable but not surprising absentee was Del. Sandra's brief marriage was falling apart by then, largely because the two had different interests. Although they both liked sports, he preferred volleyball, while she devoted herself to curling. While she skipped in the Scott, he vacationed in Hawaii.

"Definitely they had different interests," Jan said. "Neither one of them supported the other."

A private person by nature despite her increasingly public profile, Sandra tried to keep her marriage problems to herself, although occasionally she would make a passing comment about it to Bev Kozar.

"I'd never ask her for more information because that's just not the kind of person she was," Bev said. "She would tell you something and you'd be thankful she shared what little bit she did. I always just left it at that."

But about once a month Sandra would telephone her sister Carol in Calgary, the hurt apparent in her voice.

"She really didn't want to talk about it a lot," Carol recalled. "She was sad, her relationship was really falling apart."

In its first trip to the Scott, the Peterson foursome finished fourth overall, missing the playoffs after a tiebreaking loss to Ontario's Heather Houston. Looking back on that first tournament, Jan said: "We were just happy to be there. We never talked about goals. We didn't talk about anything. We just sort of went there, showed up, and played and lost a tiebreaker. [Afterwards] I think we thought we could have done a lot better if we had set the bar a little higher."

In the summer of 1991, Brian McCusker and Joan Inglis married, while Sandra's marriage moved closer towards its ultimate demise. Sandra's dreams of returning to the Scott in 1992 came up short, as her team lost to Michelle Schneider's foursome in the provincial women's final. The Schneider foursome finished fourth in the Scott, but it proved to be successful for Kathy Fahlman, Sandra's one-time skip. Kathy won all-star third honours in the Scott, affirming that she felt she was in a different psychological space, playing to win instead of just being happy to be there. She admittedly lifted some "mental monkeys" off her back.

The loss in the provincial final prompted Sandra's team to take a long look at itself.

"It made us step back and realize how badly we wanted it and that we were going to have to work really, really hard if we wanted to get back [to the Scott]," Marcia said.

That same spring, Sandra and Del separated. They divorced a year later.

"She was totally devastated by [the breakup]. She didn't have any family [in Regina] and felt like a failure because Sandra succeeded at things," Shirley said. "She didn't fail at things, so this was devastating. It was a very difficult time in her life."

Sandra addressed that in *Gold on Ice*, the book written about her team after its Olympic victory.

"My self-esteem probably hit an all-time low [after the marriage broke up]," she said. "I always thought that by the time I turned 30, I would be happily married with one or two kids. I went through the pain of divorce and started to feel like a loser — single, unattached and no prospects on the horizon. I threw myself into curling and in a sense it became my sanctuary. I practised a lot, studied game tapes of our team but also of other teams I admired. It was horrible for my personal life, but turned out great for my curling game, although that was never the plan."

On Top of the World

I n 1992, Sandra received a promotion when she was hired to
be the supervisor of the newly opened South East Leisure
Centre. Little did the city of Regina, which hired her, realize
that the supervisor was about to promote herself to the highest
plateau in women's curling worldwide.

Still aching from their loss in the provincial final in the
1991–92 season, Sandra, Jan, Joan, and Marcia decided to work
hard to win the Saskatchewan crown again. They had some ago-
nizingly bad luck on and off the ice in spiels in the fall of 1992.
In the Regina Ladies' Bonspiel, they started with a makeshift

lineup that included only three players. Sandra arrived late because she was the victim of a hit-and-run accident. Joan, who had recently delivered her first child, Rory, whom she was breast-feeding, started and finished off the game skipping. When Sandra arrived, she decided to play, even though the team felt it could manage without her. Typical of Sandra's competitiveness, she felt she could in fact "sweep away" the effects of the car accident rather than stand around and stiffen up, so she took another spot in the rotation.

The team lost the final, but it later began an incredible run, going undefeated in eight games leading up to the provincial round-robin in Shaunavon. The Peterson foursome easily beat Saskatoon's Sherry Scheirich in the final to earn another trip to the Scott and a chance to make its first of many historical championships.

Before heading off to Brandon, Manitoba, for the Scott, the team added Anita Ford as its fifth player and coach. Teams are allowed to bring a coach and an alternate player called a fifth, who can fill in for one of the four regulars. Some teams actually bring five players and rotate them to give each of them a chance to play and be prepared. Anita subsequently became the team's regular coach, while her daughter, Atina, inherited the alternate role.

The new Saskatchewan champions came to the Scott poised and prepared. Unlike in 1991, they realized if they aimed a little higher, a championship could be theirs. But they were up against some strong opposition, including defending champion Connie Laliberte; Manitoba rival Maureen Bonar; 1991

Canadian champion Julie Sutton of British Columbia; and 1982 champion Colleen Jones of Nova Scotia. A couple of other notables were Alberta's Shannon Kleibrink and Ontario's Anne Merklinger, both of whom played pivotal roles in Sandra's curling career and personal life in later years.

Brandon is in the heart of curling country and the knowledgeable and appreciative fans packed the Keystone Centre, the arena in which the event was taking place. Sandra's team finished first overall in the round-robin with a 9–2 record — losing only to Quebec's Agnes Charette and Kleibrink — and earned a bye to the final.

Ontario's Pat Reid, who worked closely with Sandra's team in future years as a liaison for the Canadian Curling Association and the Canadian Olympic Association, noticed a big change in Sandra from her first appearance in the Scott two years before. Pat thought Sandra seemed a bit nervous and unsure of herself back then, but this time she had the look of a champion, a kind of "get out of my way" attitude.

"I think of [Chrysler boss] Lee Iacocca in his ad: lead, follow, or get out of the way. That was Sandra," Pat said. "She was there and she was leading and everyone else could just jump on board with her. She was very committed, very determined when she got to Brandon. She had a confidence that was lacking the first time out, I think."

Jan agreed there was a change in Sandra and in the team, but noted they were a more experienced group in 1993.

In the semi-final, Brandon's Maureen Bonar beat Anne Merklinger 8–4 to face Sandra. The Regina foursome faced a capacity crowd of 5,331 principally rooting for the hometown team, but a contingent from Saskatchewan offered the Regina quartet plenty of support. The score was tied at six heading into the final end and Sandra had hammer (last-rock advantage). On her final rock, she faced a Manitoba stone in the top of the 12-foot and had two options. She could remove the opposition stone and hope to score a point by saving her shooter (final stone) anywhere in the rings, or she could ignore the opposition stone and draw closer to the button. She elected to play the hit, a move that is the safer of the two shots because sometimes a draw shot can fail to slow down, rolling too far. With the pressure of a Canadian championship on the line, which can cause some players to overthrow or underthrow depending on how they handle anxiety and adrenalin, Sandra made it look easy. She removed the opposition rock and easily saved her shooter in the rings to collect one point and win 7–6. Sandra started crying tears of joy.

The girl from Biggar recorded her biggest win and the first national women's title for Saskatchewan since Marj Mitchell's in 1980. Similar to Sandra, Marj Mitchell played out of the Caledonian Club.

Sandra wiped her tears away and joined her teammates at the other end of the sheet. At the closing banquet that night, Sandra received the all-star skip award for the first time, yet the occasion was also important for another reason. It was here that the first meeting took place between the Regina foursome and Vancouver's Lindsay Sparkes. Lindsay had played in the national tournament four times between 1979 and 1986, and had won two titles, one as a skip. Lindsay had been scaling the national coaching ladder in the '90s, and in 1992 the Canadian Curling Association appointed her to be team leader for the women's squads in the world championships and head coach for the 1998 Olympic team. She had played against Sandra and Jan when they were part of Kathy Fahlman's team in the 1987 Olympic Trials. Lindsay really didn't know them personally, but quickly bonded with Sandra and Jan and their two teammates whose great sense of humour played a key role in their growth as the greatest women's team in curling history.

With the Scott tournament win captured, Sandra now turned her attention to her next challenge: the world championship, coming up in Geneva, Switzerland, a month later. The worlds involve 10 teams from North America, Europe, and the Pacific Rim. The competition is a nine-game round-robin followed by two semi-finals and a final. The competition is usually not as strong on paper as the Canadian nationals because of the lack of players per capita in the other countries. In fact, some teams outside of North America come to Canada in the fall to find competition they are lacking at home. Because of its dominance in the sport, Canada annually goes into the worlds as the favourite or one of the favourites and expectations are high. While some Canadian players value a national championship more than a world championship because of the increased competition, the pressure from the public can be more demanding at the global level because anything short of a gold medal can be considered a disappointment.

That's one of the reasons why the Canadian Curling

Association decided to help its representatives by appointing a team leader who could help to facilitate any problems that may arise in world championship play. Lindsay quickly realized the newly crowned Canadian champions already had their minds on the world championships and they welcomed any help.

"I was immediately taken by their openness to my presence and any way I could help them in their goal to win the world championship," Lindsay said. "I was very comfortable. I really felt I could say whatever I needed to say and I could use that to make them stronger."

In preparation, Sandra watched videotapes to learn as much as she could about the Free Guard Zone rules the International Curling Federation adopted for the world championships. The new rules allowed teams to create more offence by limiting the removal of the first four stones if they were placed outside the rings. The more rocks in play made it more exciting to watch because the team with last-rock advantage could not play con-servatively and repeatedly remove opposition rocks. The rule essentially allowed the opposition to steal points even if they didn't have last-rock advantage by manufacturing ways to reach the button. Similar to playing pool or billiards, it required skill and understanding of the angles. Some Canadian critics argued that the Free Guard Zone rules tilted the playing field in favour of the Europeans because they had already adopted the format while the Canadians essentially had to learn a new style.

Coincidentally, the reigning Canadian men's champion of the time, Russ Howard of Ontario, had pioneered the format. He and his brother, Glenn, who played third on Team Howard,

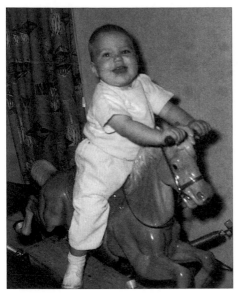

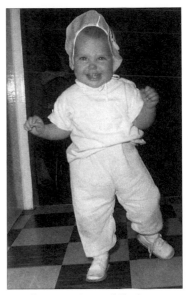

Ride 'em, cowgirl: Sandra, in 1964, at home in Biggar, Saskatchewan.

Proud parents, Art and Shirley Schmirler, capture one-year-old Sandra's first steps.

Sandra and her two good "friends," Mrs. Beasley and Cheeky.

That winning smile:
Seven-year-old
Sandra poses happily
for this photograph.

The Schmirler family, Christmas 1975. Clockwise from back left: Art, Beverley, Carol, Sandra (holding family dog Cookie), and Shirley.

Eight-year-old Sandra with her mom. (Sandra had just about every Brownie badge possible.)

Sandra replying to a toast from the teachers at her high-school graduation.

It's a family affair: The 1986 winners of the Ladies Cash Bonspiel at the Hub City Curling Club in Saskatoon. From the left: Hughene Day (Sandra's aunt), Shirley (Sandra's mom), Laurie Secord, and Sandra.

Fahlman Team at the send-off to Canadian Scott Tournament of Hearts in Lethbridge. From the left: Kathy Fahlman, Sandra, Jan Betker, and Sheila and Michelle Schneider.

Team Schmirler: Shirley (left), Sandra, Mabel McLeod (Sandra's grandmother), and Art in 1987.

Saskatchewan's finest: the Fahlman team at the
1987 Scott Tournament of Hearts in Lethbridge.

"Sandra kind of stuck out because she had this wonderful delivery — even back
then she got so low — and was a real excellent shotmaker." — Laurie Humble

which was then one of the pre-eminent teams in the world, experimented with the rules for years to make their practices more challenging.

The Canadian women finished the round-robin in third place with a 7–2 record. In the semi-final, the Canadians faced defending champion Elisabet Gustafson of Sweden, whose team had won the round-robin match 10–3 in seven ends. The Canadians rebounded to beat Sweden 10–7. In the other semi-final, Germany's Janet Clews-Strayer, a transplanted Canadian from Regina, beat two-time world champion Dordi Nordby of Norway. The final pitted a current resident from the Queen City of Regina against a former resident, but the big question was who would wear the crown when the game ended? Clews-Strayer came into the game upset about a personnel decision made by her coach concerning the lead player, who had rotated with the alternate all season. The Canadians played the Germans hard right from the outset. The Germans struggled throughout the match, forcing their skip repeatedly to bail them out. When Canada scored two points to lead 3–1 at the half, it had a comfortable cushion. Germany narrowed it down to one in the sixth, after which the teams traded single points in each of the next three ends. Canada forced Germany to concede when it could not score two in the final frame.

The Canadian women experienced joy and relief, knowing they did not have to go home and explain a defeat. If a team loses, it has to spend the balance of the year — and possibly an entire career — explaining why.

"That Maple Leaf in curling is a sign of representing the most successful curling nation in the world," Sandra said in *Gold on Ice*. "You are so proud to wear it and you don't want to let down the curling fans back home."

That year the Canadian curlers brought home a double championship — Russ Howard's team scored a 10–4 victory over Scotland's David Smith. There would be no explanations of losses needed this year.

The Canadian women received a hero's welcome upon their return to Regina. They rode in a horse-drawn carriage to their hometown club, the Callie, while thousands of people cheered the procession. Sandra received a massive celebration in Biggar.

Sandra was becoming a star. She received a mention in *Sports Illustrated*'s "Faces in the Crowd," which is a small section profiling athletes from different amateur sports. She also did a milk commercial with four Canadian world champions from other sports. She used some of the money for corrective work on her teeth, notably the two she chipped in her youth.

Sandra had a gold medal and commercial opportunities, but she lacked a partner with whom she could share her success. She felt like a third wheel when she socialized with her curling friends, who were either married or in serious relationships. Then she found the man of her dreams — Shannon England — in a curling club, compliments of Marcia, who played the role of matchmaker.

"Everybody was always looking for somebody to set up Sandra with," Marcia said with a smile. "We were bugging her that her hormones were raging and it was time."

Shannon grew up in Moose Jaw, 40 miles from Regina, and had been a classmate of Marcia's in the two-year data processing program at Saskatchewan Technical Institute. Shannon was also a competitive curler, playing mostly at the club level. Shannon had heard a little about Sandra in 1991, but hadn't been as involved in curling at the time. As a fan in 1993, he followed the fortunes of Sandra's team a little more closely.

When Sandra's team had been eliminated from the spiel, Marcia manoeuvred Sandra over to the glass to watch Shannon's team, which was playing its final game. Shannon and his younger brother, Curt, were standing at the other end, and Sandra asked Marcia which of the two she wanted her to see. Then, in a moment typical of Sandra's quick wit, she added: "Uh, it doesn't matter. Either one will do."

When Shannon's team finished its game, Marcia introduced him to Sandra, who was sitting at a table with the Swedish team of Peter Lindholm. The Canadians had met the Swedes earlier that year at the worlds, and Lindholm's team had come to Canada to play in some spiels.

"A bunch of us were up in the bar that night and everybody had had quite a bit to drink," Marcia said. "Shannon was kind of sitting around waiting to talk to her after I talked to him about her. I kept saying to him, 'I don't know if this is such a good night,' because everybody was having such a good time and everybody was drinking lots, but he just sat there and waited for the opportunity to talk to her."

"Sandra had had a few paralyzers by then — she wasn't

feeling any pain at all," Shannon recalled. "We played a little shuffleboard and just did a little talking. I drove her home that night."

Sandra phoned her sister Carol the next morning to talk about the date. Although she thought he was a nice fellow, she said, "He doesn't make my heart go kaboom kaboom." Nevertheless, she wanted Carol's opinion about inviting Shannon over to watch the Blue Jays' American League playoff game on television that day. Sandra loved sports but figured Shannon would be watching the game with friends. Carol encouraged her to give him a call. Carol knew that Sandra was still feeling low about her failed marriage and thought nobody was going to like her again. While Sandra procrastinated, Shannon called and invited her to his home for supper and to watch the game.

"I cooked her a nice meal," Shannon said. "I made chicken Kiev from scratch with glazed carrots and baked potato or something like that. I was just trying to impress the hell out of her."

Within only a few weeks, the two knew they belonged together. They had similar likes: sports, working around the yard, going out for supper, and family unity. In addition, both had experienced failed marriages, although at that time Shannon's divorce had not been finalized. Both were aware of the difference between their first marriages and how they felt in this relationship.

Like the line "you complete me" from the movie *Jerry Maguire*, Sandra had found her special someone. She had gone from a rocky marriage to a relationship revolving around rocks, because of their mutual love of curling.

Shirley had some concerns because Shannon was so freshly out of his marriage. She had also had some uncertainties before Sandra's first marriage, but had kept her opinions to herself at the time.

"I didn't keep my mouth shut this time," Shirley recalled proudly. "I said, 'Is he on the rebound? You make sure he isn't on the rebound.' I did a lot of yapping. I did it to him as well. At the same time, Sandra was going to do what she wanted to do anyway, like she did the first time, too."

A Magnificent Run

Despite their loss against curlers of inferior talent in the warm-up bonspiel to start the season, the defending champions otherwise had a solid fall, earning $30,000 on the cashspiel circuit with wins in Kelowna, British Columbia; Thunder Bay, Ontario; Saskatoon; and Berne, Switzerland. The collective earnings were considered quite good, given that women didn't have the same cash opportunities as the men (and still are not even close to being on par). The two-week trip to Berne served as a working holiday in preparation for the team's defence of its national title.

As the team started the curling year, the romance between Sandra and Shannon also progressed. Shannon travelled to a couple of the western spiels and slowly started to fit in with the other members of Sandra's team and their partners — Kerry Gudereit, Brian McCusker, and Frank Macera. Shannon joined the entourage for the 1994 Scott tournament in Kitchener, Ontario.

The tournament that year was memorable for a couple of reasons. First, Sandra's team dressed in kilts instead of pants and had the red and white colours of Team Canada instead of the traditional green of Saskatchewan. Second, the team had a boisterous contingent, which can best be described as the Rat Pack. The champions had a good-luck charm: a squashed rubber rat given to Sandra by one of her colleagues the year before. Jan bought some toy rats that squeaked and gave them to the team's supporters, who included Art and Shirley, Shannon, and friends and family of the other team members. The Rat Pack had ample opportunity to make noise as the champions made road kill out of their opponents, finishing the round robin with a 10–1 record and a bye to the final. Its only loss came against Manitoba's Connie Laliberte, who had been dubbed the Ice Queen many years before because of her stoical demeanour on the ice. Connie advanced to the final by beating Sherry Anderson from Prince Albert, Saskatchewan, in the semi-final.

The final featured a close battle in which Manitoba led 3–2 after seven ends. Team Canada had the last-rock advantage at that point and played patiently, waiting for the opportunity to score at least two points. It didn't materialize in the next two ends, so Team Canada headed into the final end looking to score. Sandra had a chance to make three points with her last shot but needed to remove the opposition stone sitting wide open in the button, without deflecting it into two Team Canada stones sitting behind it. Everything needed to be perfect.

The Canadians executed it with textbook perfection as the Manitoba stone sailed practically straight through the two Canadian rocks in behind like a croquet ball going through a wicket. Sandra leapt into the air and raised her arms in celebration, then dropped to her knees and began to cry.

The Canadians headed off to Oberstdorf, Germany, a month later for the worlds, but there was a key moment before the tournament began when Sandra addressed Lindsay Sparkes with a concern.

"How do we keep it alive so that we can be the team that represents Canada in the Olympics?" she asked.

Sandra had already begun focusing on that Olympic gold — four years away.

But first there was another world championship to win. The Canadians lost only one game in the round-robin, dropping a 6–3 decision to Denmark's Helena Blach-Lavrsen in the middle of the week. Team Canada faced Scotland in the final and won 5–3 to record its second consecutive global title, something no Canadian men's or women's team had ever done.

••••••

Shannon had travelled to the world championships to support Sandra in her latest glory. After the 1994 season, Shannon moved in with Sandra, who had maintained possession of the house as part of her settlement with Del. Art and Shirley Schmirler jokingly referred to Shannon as their sin-in-law because he and Sandra weren't married. In reality, Shannon spent a lot of time alone because of Sandra's busy public-speaking schedule.

"The lady was never around," Shannon recalled with a laugh. "I was actually kind of lonely a bit there the first year because she was gone so much. But every time she was home, we were always together and doing stuff."

Success showed its rewards in other ways. Along with speaking engagements, the team had opportunities to play in golf tournaments and cash in on sponsorship offers from individuals or companies seeking to link their names to the two-time world champions. The team initially employed local agents to coordinate their engagements but eventually settled on doing it themselves. And it became a problem. The increased time spent on business meant less time was spent with their partners and families.

"It was getting very tough for them," Shannon said. "As much fun as it is to win, it's also very demanding, so going into the Scott that year [1995] in Calgary they weren't mentally ready to want to win."

The champions' magnificent run finally ended when they finished third in the tournament, won by Connie Laliberte, who beat Alberta's Cathy Borst 6–5 in the final. The Albertans had had to play in tiebreakers to qualify for the playoffs, and after beating Team Canada 7–5 in the semi-final they ran out of gas playing their fifth game in about 26 hours.

Finishing third with an 8–3 record might have been accept-
able to some teams, but to Sandra's it was unacceptable.

"Even though we finished third, we felt it was a disaster," Jan
said. "We knew that had we prepared properly things could have
been different."

"They were just mentally tired," said Shannon. "It was a long,
fun, crazy two years. They were a little more antsy and cranky
and not themselves out there. They still tried their best to get
back, but I knew they were tired."

The team called on Lindsay Sparkes to spend a weekend with
them in the summer, partly to go over what went wrong in
Calgary. Sandra made the call to Lindsay and said she hadn't
told anyone outside of the team about the proposed summit.

"The girls shared a lot; they were so open and honest," Lindsay
said. "That was a true, intimate bonding we all went through. We
socialized with the husbands, but our time together was pretty
heavy duty. We spent a lot of time just looking at every little
thing that made them a team and what made them perform and
really looked at it critically. Their openness and honesty, I think,
really helped point them in the right direction again."

In the 1995–96 season, the team made some lineup changes
— some expected and some unexpected. Joan took the season
off to have her second child and was temporarily replaced by
Pam Bryden. But the changes affected the chemistry of the
team and it did not have the success it enjoyed in the past.
Sandra missed Joan's spirited cheerleading and talking, and her
confidence eroded.

In late November, the situation reached a critical stage. In only two weeks, the team was going to face Connie Laliberte's squad in Thunder Bay in a best-of-three playoff. The winner would earn a berth in the 1997 Olympic Trials. To address her faltering confidence, Sandra met with Jan, Marcia, and Joan, who would join the team for the best-of-three series.

"Sandra wasn't getting the response she usually got when she came down the ice to throw," Marcia said. "You miss a few and you start questioning yourself. Pam is a great girl, but she's quiet. The team was struggling and Sandra was having trouble with that."

Joan surmised that Sandra's inability to recover from the defeat in the 1995 Scott tournament was also a factor in her dilemma.

"You put all that together and she was really in a bad mental state," Joan said. "She was just a mess from the start of the year. I remember the team all called me separately saying, 'We need you to come and help because Sandra's in a really bad mental spot.' That was the first time anybody had walked away since we put the team together — even though mine was a maternity leave — and we realized that the combination of the four people was what made it special. A piece of the puzzle was missing when I went, and as it turned out it was a fairly big piece. I'm the one that always got people talking and communicating and recognizing or saying out loud, 'This is a problem and let's work it out.'"

Sandra wanted to lessen her psychological and emotional strain by turning over the skipping chores to Jan, but Jan did not want the role and neither did either of the other two. That's when Joan found the right words to ease the situation for her strained skip.

"I remember specifically saying over and over, 'What is the worst thing that can happen, Sandra? Tell me what could happen if we lost and you played terribly? What would happen after that? The sun will come up, right? No one will hold a grudge.'"

They realized their success and friendship had been based on doing things together and supporting one another when things didn't work.

"That was our first lesson in a very special relationship that the four of us had and were able to bring out in each other," Joan said. "That was the first time it really became evident that we relied on each other a lot to help us through those things."

"I think that meeting really settled Sandra down," Marcia said. "It took her a couple of days, so by the time we went to play in that best-of-three series, she played really well. I think she realized everything wasn't on her shoulders, plus she had Joan back for that best-of-three and I think she felt really good after that."

Connie Laliberte's team and Sandra's team split the first two games, but Sandra's foursome prevailed in the final, the first big step in the path to the Olympics in February 1998. To reach that goal, the team had to win the Trials in November 1997, but there remained lots of curling well before that.

The team qualified for the provincial championship but had all kinds of problems in the tournament. Marcia was too sick to play, so the team recruited local curler Karen Daku, who formed the front end with Pam Bryden, who subbed for Joan. Jan, meanwhile, had trouble sleeping because she was pregnant. Despite a valiant effort, the makeshift lineup couldn't beat Sherry Scheirich's team from Saskatoon in the final. Scheirich proved the win was no fluke as she guided her team to a fourth-place finish in one of the toughest Scott tournaments in years, which was won by Ontario's Marilyn Bodogh.

Team Schmirler

Sandra had more than just curling on her mind in 1996. After two and a half years of living together, she and Shannon decided to strengthen their love for one another in marriage. For two people so deeply in love, they didn't exactly punctuate it with a proposal that moved heaven and earth. In fact, the decision was kind of nonchalant.

"Because we had both gone through it once, it wasn't terribly romantic," Shannon confessed. "I think we just both talked to each other and said, 'Should we do it? Yeah.'"

They chose June 22, 1996, as their date and opted for a small service in the backyard of their home. A justice of the peace performed the rituals, witnessed only by Shannon's father, stepmother, brother, and sister-in-law, and Art and Shirley. The following day, Jan played host to a party for the newlyweds. A family barbecue capped off the celebrations the following weekend.

Sandra decided to keep her maiden name for business and curling purposes, which did not bother Shannon, illustrating the support he had for her. Sandra had wanted to shed the name Peterson after her first marriage ended and use her maiden name, but it simplified things to maintain her married name when the team started winning provincial and national championships. From 1996 onward, she became Sandra Schmirler. In less than a year after her wedding, she was tagged with the nickname "Schmirler the Curler" because it just seemed to fit. Most curling fans didn't realize this nickname had been conferred on her some 15 years before, by her former boss Bev Kozar at the North West Leisure Centre.

Shannon and Sandra also decided it was the right time to begin their own family. He was 29, and Sandra, at 30, really wanted to be a mother. All her teammates had at least one child by now, and Sandra wanted to fulfill that part of her life. It proved to be difficult. Sandra required surgery to remove fibroids lining her uterus. These non-cancerous growths can cause bleeding or interfere with the ability to become pregnant, but surgery can help correct the problem. Sandra's operation in September was complicated by the proximity of the fibroids to major blood vessels.

Once Sandra and Shannon were given the medical go-ahead by the doctors, they began their attempts to have a child. Sandra considered putting off attempts to become pregnant because it could complicate the team's curling schedule, particularly the Olympic Trials.

"We were the ones who said, 'Don't be stupid, go [for it]. There's more to life than curling,'" Jan said.

Sandra began a diary of thoughts to her future daughter shortly thereafter.

"Your dad and I were given the OK to start trying to make you around the end of Dec/96. Well, guess what . . . it was a very successful New Year's Eve. More on this later."

Sandra sensed she was pregnant while playing in the provincials in Swift Current in the third week of January.

"I was excited at the thought but was scared to believe it in case it wasn't true," she wrote in her diary. "I wasn't going to take a pregnancy test until the tournament was over, so now I was very excited to go home and find out for real."

Sandra's team won the tournament and when she returned home she learned Shannon's competitive curling team had been doing well in the southern part of the Saskatchewan men's play-downs. Sandra went to the Wheat City Club to congratulate him and ordered a paralyzer drink, hoping it would be her last for a very long time if she was indeed pregnant.

She stopped off at the drug store to pick up a pregnancy test and then headed home. The test clearly showed she was pregnant.

"Believe it or not, I was quite calm," she wrote. "I smiled, cried a bit, and was very eager for Daddy to get home."

Sandra left the test result by the sink and Shannon noticed it when he went to the bathroom before going to bed. He immediately began to worry.

"I was petrified to be a father," he said. "Kids weren't part of my life. It was just my brother and me. I didn't have any older brothers or sisters. I was totally naive. Sandra really wanted to be a parent, and I knew it would be fine once I had to go through it, but it still scared the crap out of me to be a father."

Sandra and Shannon made an emotional decision at that time to sell their home from her first marriage. Sandra wrote about it in her diary to her future daughter.

"Dad had to convince me for a few days but the more I thought about it, the better the idea sounded. I realized this was a great chance to put the total past behind and to really start a new life with you and daddy."

• • • • • •

The 1997 Scott tournament took place in Vancouver in February. The lineup included defending champion Marilyn Bodogh of Ontario, 1990 Canadian champion Alison Goring of Ontario, Alberta's Cathy Borst, hometown favourite Kelley Owen, Nova Scotia's perennial champion Colleen Jones, Manitoba's Janet Harvey, and P.E.I.'s Rebecca Jean MacPhee. Overall, the field appeared to be one of the strongest in years.

The day before the tournament began, the team participated in the annual Ford Hot Shots, a skills competition in which the winner receives a car. While standing next to Marilyn Bodogh before they undertook the skills drill, Sandra whispered to her longtime friend that she was pregnant.

"They were the nicest words I'd heard come out of her throughout our whole relationship because to me the ultimate is giving birth and giving life," Marilyn said. "I immediately turned around and hugged her. Of course everyone said, 'What's going on?' because she had tears and I had tears. I told her I wouldn't tell anybody. Of course, I didn't have to. She told everybody."

Normally a pregnancy is not a big deal to the media, but it became an interesting sidebar because motherhood was already part of the Team Schmirler storyline. One writer suggested that if Sandra was suffering from morning sickness, she should be renamed Schmirler the Hurler. It became a running joke, even used by Shannon.

Team Schmirler opened with a 9–2 win over Marilyn Bodogh but lost two of its next three matches. It did not lose a game the remainder of the way, beating Ontario's Alison Goring 8–5 in the final. Neither skip played particularly well, but Saskatchewan's overall experience played a major role in the outcome.

Marilyn, for one, watched this curling powerhouse in awe.

"I remember standing back and saying, 'God, they are so good. How do you get that good? How do you get that lucky to get that good? There's got to be a reason why they're getting picked.'"

The Canadian champions travelled to Berne, Switzerland, a month later for the world championships. Sandra had an ultrasound beforehand and it looked great — so much so that

Sandra proudly displayed it to her teammates when they pulled out their baby shots. The Canadians finished first in the round-robin, beating Denmark 5–2 in one semi-final. Norway beat Japan 12–5 in the other semi to face the Canadians in the final. After Canada scored a whopping five points in the fifth end to go up 6–1, it was all over but for the handshakes to end the game. That happened when Canada ran Norway out of rocks to win 8–4. This win marked the first time a men's or women's team from any country had won three world championships.

· · · · · ·

In May, Sandra and Shannon moved into a new house and prepared for the birth of their first child. Because of her previous fibroid surgery, Sandra's doctors determined she should have a caesarean section a couple of weeks before full term. A natural delivery could have been risky.

An ultrasound in July showed that everything was progressing well. It also indicated that Sandra was carrying a girl. Another test determined the date to do the operation, September 15. Sandra hardly slept the night before the surgery because she was so excited.

Following the C-section the next morning, Shannon stood next to Sandra, holding her hand.

As Sandra wrote in her diary, "You made your way out and they said 'You've got a girl.' Well, I knew who you were but I was still very excited. Tears came to my eyes as I finally realized the greatest moment of my life, the birth of our daughter. They wrapped you up quickly and then gave you to Dad. I couldn't hold you right away because they still needed to finish the operation. You only stayed with us for a few minutes then Dad took you to the nursery for some hospital procedures. We met up together in recovery. I was in awe of you. So perfect. So beautiful, a dream come true. Daddy and I are so proud. We called everyone from recovery, the thrill in everyone's voice was wonderful to hear. Sara, you really are a precious gift."

Shannon said he and Sandra sifted through a whole bunch of names before settling on Sara Marion.

"Sara really didn't mean anything for us other than it was a nice, simple, strong name," he said. "It was just something we liked. The middle name is for my mother."

In the next months, Sara became the most famous curling baby in the world.

"My Best Delivery"

It did not take Sandra long to recover from childbirth, much to the surprise of her mother, who had come to stay with her for the first week.

"We walked, we shopped, we did everything," Shirley said. "You'd never dream she'd had a caesarean. I said, 'How ya doing?' and she said, 'I'm kind of tired because nobody told me to lie down.' I said, 'Sandra, you have to stop and rest,' so she listened."

Sandra really didn't have a lot of time for lying down, though. She had to play in the biggest Canadian tournament in history

— the Olympic Trials — in Brandon, Manitoba, November 22–30. The tournament pitted ten men's and ten women's teams, selected from a series of qualifiers. Not only was this expected to be the toughest lineup ever assembled for the Trials, but the prize carried added value. The winner had a chance to play in the Olympics in which curling had become a full-medal sport instead of a demonstration sport.

The Schmirler team tuned up for the Trials with three separate tournaments, winning the first and the third but reaching only the semi-finals in the one in between. The team fell short against Alberta's Shannon Kleibrink, whose quartet from Calgary did not have a big profile on the national scene, but that was about to change.

To be with Sara as long as possible, Sandra took her to the Trials, accompanied by her father and a host of relatives. Sandra maintained her nursing duties, sometimes between games, and admitted in her diary it was a very challenging week.

"You were such a good baby. By this point you had been sleeping through the night, so really having you at the Trials was a breeze."

The curling, however, was not a breeze, because of the mental pressure of having to play one tough team after another. The women's teams included Team Schmirler, Manitoba's Connie Laliberte, Ontario's Marilyn Bodogh, Saskatchewan's Sherry Scheirich, Nova Scotia's Mary Mattatall, Ontario's Anne Merklinger, Alberta's Cathy Borst, Ontario's Alison Goring, B.C.'s Kelley Law, and Alberta's Shannon Kleibrink. Never before had there been a women's field with this much depth — sometimes in the Scott Tournament of Hearts there is a tendency to downplay some teams because they come from a province or territory without a lot of serious competition. Practically all the pundits picked Sandra's team to win.

Team Schmirler finished the round-robin first overall at 7–2, losing only to Cathy Borst and Marilyn Bodogh, neither of whom qualified for the playoffs. Sandra's team earned a bye to the final by placing first, but had to wait two days to play the game. In the semi-final, Shannon Kleibrink beat Kelley Law 7–4, setting up a match that would be remembered for the shot heard round the curling world.

As the final unfolded, the teams engaged in a fairly tight contest in which the Albertans led 4–3 after six ends. They appeared poised for a steal of one point in the seventh with a stone buried in the button. To fall behind by two points this late in the match would have made it difficult even for a team as good as Sandra's. Sandra had one stone directly in the top of the four-foot and another directly in behind. Shannon Kleibrink had only one plan in mind: to keep the centre-line guarded to prevent Sandra from making an incredible shot — a circus shot, as they say in curling — that could extricate the buried stone in the button. Shannon appeared to have done that with her last shot, but she had left Sandra a smidgen of a chance to remove the buried stone. Sandra had a rock sitting in the corner of the top of the 12-foot from her previous shot. Sandra and Jan saw the possibility of the circus shot happening before Shannon

Kleibrink had opted to play the guard, but like cagey card players, they did not tip their hand. They had an ace, albeit a low-percentage one, to play.

Anne Merklinger, who worked on the telecast of the game for the Canadian Broadcasting Corporation, pointed out the possibility of the potential highlight-reel shot to the national audience. Lindsay Sparkes, appointed by the Canadian Curling Association to accompany the winning team to the Olympics as head coach, anxiously sat in the sponsors' lounge, watching the game on television. Lindsay wanted Sandra's team to win because of her connection to it since the first world championship victory in 1993, but as the end shaped up, she hastily began making notes and planning for the post-game meeting with Shannon Kleibrink's squad.

Meanwhile, to have any chance at the shot stone, Sandra needed to carom her shooter off her own stone and angle in perfectly to tap out the opposition rock in the button. It's called a hit and roll and takeout or a cross the house angle takeout, although shots of these kind often lend themselves to a variety of more fanciful expressions. Team Schmirler had shown its mastery too many times to make disbelievers out of the capacity crowd in the Keystone Centre and the hundreds of thousands watching the game on television.

Sandra delivered the rock, and Joan and Marcia swept it perfectly while Jan called the line. Sandra stayed on top of the shot from her end, urging on Joan and Marcia with her skipping signals. Quality sweepers such as Joan and Marcia develop an understanding of when to apply the broom to the ice to help advance the stone and when to back off. However, the urging from the skip can be as much an emotional lift as it is a simple command. And, when Sandra started barking out signals, her voice sounded like a combination of a shriek and a squeak. Sandra's rock hit the stone perfectly at the top of the 12-foot and angled in directly to tap the stone off the button and take its place. It was a Minnesota Fats special. Combined with the two stones she already had surrounding the rock in the button, Sandra counted three points. Instead of trailing 5–3 going into the eighth end, Team Schmirler led 6–4. Pandemonium prevailed among the crowd after Sandra's shot, while the skip reacted with unbridled delight, jumping up and down as if she'd already won the game.

"Those of us who knew Sandra knew the bigger shot you left her, the more likely she was to make it," Anne Merklinger said. "I got to see that from a different perspective than many people who might have been sitting in the arena or watching it on TV thinking, 'There's no way.'"

"It was like the curling gods were shining on us because it worked to perfection," Sandra wrote in her diary. "This really turned the game in our favour."

With Sandra standing alone at the far end, hyperventilating following her miraculous shot, Jan, the savvy veteran, took control and reminded Joan and Marcia there were still three ends to be played and they still had a challenging task ahead of them. The Free Guard Zone rules made it impossible to sit on a lead.

Shannon Kleibrink scored two in the eighth to tie the game, but Sandra seized an opportunity in the ninth and scored three.

This time it was all but over. In the final end, Joan displayed why she is one of the top players in the world by making a marvellous takeout with her second shot to clear the house of all the Kleibrink stones. The crowd erupted with appreciative applause, recognizing the awesome shot. Shannon was run out of rocks and Team Schmirler recorded one of its most notable victories.

When it ended, Sandra rushed over to her husband, who was holding Sara in his arms, and cried — tears of joy and sadness.

"The first thought that came to mind was excitement — we're going to the Olympics. My next thought was of you, Sara. My God, I thought, I have to leave you. At this moment, it broke my heart. I found it very difficult to ever imagine leaving you. This feeling took over and I couldn't fight back the tears."

Once she had time to gather her thoughts after the game, Sandra made one of the most memorable remarks in curling history when asked about the shot in the seventh end.

"That ranks up to probably the biggest shot I've ever made," Sandra said. "Sara was my best delivery, but that was pretty close."

The closing ceremonies took a long time and Sandra wanted to feed Sara, but first Sandra had to go to the Doping Control Centre to provide a urine sample. That was when it really hit home that curling was part of the Olympics.

"Daddy brought you over to the Doping Control so I could feed you and spend time with you. It didn't take me long to pee but it sure took Auntie Joan [McCusker] a long time."

Going for the Gold

The Olympics were only nine weeks away and Team Schmirler had a busy schedule ahead. Not only did it play three warm-up tournaments and some local games to prepare for the Games, but it also had to deal with numerous media demands. If reporters called Sandra at home, she'd pass the requests along to the Canadian Curling Association, which was overseeing the interviews. This arrangement had been made with the CCA to allow Sandra's team to concentrate on their preparations and to deal with family matters.

Before leaving for the Olympics, the Canadian teams

headed to Calgary, where they would be outfitted with clothing sponsored by Roots. The time leading up to the trip to Calgary became harder for Sandra, knowing she would have to part with Sara.

Because Shannon and the other spouses would be joining their wives in Japan, Sara needed a sitter at home. Sandra and Shannon decided to send Sara to stay with her aunt, Carol, who lived 40 miles outside Calgary. However much Sandra valued the opportunity to play in the Olympics and represent her country, she had a hard time separating herself from her beloved Sara. Shannon tried to ease her anguish by telling her, "It's such a small window in Sara's life. She won't even remember it. Two weeks isn't that big. You're going to the Olympics. It's not going to be that bad. You're leaving your baby with your sister, so don't feel bad about doing this. Not many people get this kind of opportunity."

Beverley drove to the hotel where the Canadian teams were staying, to meet Sandra and take Sara to Carol's farm. Sandra buckled Sara into the car seat and tried to remain strong despite her aching heart.

"Drive carefully," Sandra said to Beverley. "I'm not going to cry. Don't even talk to me."

"Carol and I were worried about how she was going to curl because she was having such a hard time," Beverley said. "We'd ask, 'Are you practising? How are you doing with the curling?' to pump her up, but she didn't even want to talk about it. She didn't even want to think about it. All she could think about was leaving Sara behind. We were saying, 'You're going to have a good time. You're going to have a wonderful time. You're going to have experiences you're going to share with Sara,' but she didn't care. Once she was there she enjoyed it, but the actual leaving of Sara was a tough one."

"I knew this was going to be tough," she wrote in her diary. "My heart broke to leave you but I didn't really have a choice. Carol and Bev are very much looking forward to caring for you. This is what is comforting me during this big adventure away from you. Everyone says you will be proud when you get older. Daddy gave me a very special gift this Christmas — a locket to put your picture in, to keep you near my heart every moment I'm away from you and Dad. I'm wearing it now and look at it often."

The Canadian teams left February 2 for Osaka and stayed overnight before flying the following day to Nagano. Pat Reid, the women's team leader appointed by the Canadian Olympic Association, made an entry in Sandra's diary to Sara, talking about the five-year project planning and preparing Canada's teams for the Games. She mentioned how happy she was for Sandra and her teammates and hoped that all their dreams would prevail.

"Your Mom has walked the stage with Donovan Bailey, Nancy Greene and Jesse Owens," Pat wrote. "She stands eye to eye with each of them. I hope you take as much pride in your Mom's achievements as she can because I know that above all else you are the golden defining moment of her life. Your presence and your Dad's has enriched your Mom's life and inspired her."

After arriving in Nagano, the team was bused to the Olympic

curling venue in Karizawa, about an hour away. Sandra sent an e-mail to her sister Carol and asked her to give Sara a hug.

"I held a little babe today about your age. My heart yearns to be with you," she said in the e-mail.

The day after her team's arrival, Sandra experienced an emotional moment at a dinner hosted by the mayor of Karizawa. A reporter asked Sandra about Sara and it made Sandra feel sad.

"I thought about you all evening, shed a few tears and wished I was with you and your Dad. On this trip I'm really trying not to feel sorry for myself too much."

The next day the Canadian women's team and the Canadian men's team, the latter skipped by Mike Harris of Ontario, left early in the morning for Nagano to participate in a variety of functions before the opening ceremonies the following day. The day of the opening ceremonies dragged on forever for the Canadians until they finally made their procession into the Olympic stadium.

"In the entrance the hockey players start chanting 'Go Canada Go,'" Sandra wrote in her diary. "This really gets the blood going. We are announced and we walk in expecting a warm, loud reception. What we hear is polite flag flickering. It seems so quiet. It is very cool walking around looking up at some 50,000 people. Because we come in in alphabetical order, we are sitting in the arena for the entry of most of the athletes. This takes a long time because there are lots of nations taking part, some with only one or two athletes. Canada has a large contingent. The best part was the entrance of the torch carried by a disabled runner who was injured by a land mine. He lost his hand and his leg. He was surrounded by children snowlets. They are so sweet. The flame is then passed to a marathoner who runs up the huge flight of stairs. Then the best thing. Midori Ito, the figure skater, is raised up on a platform, takes the torch and lights the flame. Really neat."

The curling tournament began two days later and the Canadian women's team opened with a win against the U.S. but lost later in the day to Norway. Sandra had a chance to hold a baby in her arms because Richard Hart, the third for the Canadian men's team, and his wife had brought their son, Joey, to the Games. Joey was about two and a half months younger than Sara.

Sandra's team played Japan and won and prepared to play Denmark the following day. Shannon had arrived from Regina, which lifted Sandra's spirits, but the team encountered another "zinger" when Marcia phoned home and found out her grand-mother had died. Joan's grandmother had died while the team was in Calgary before leaving for Japan.

"Boy, we sure are being tested," Sandra wrote in her diary. "Poor Marcia. We all had a good cry. My heart goes out to her. When things like this happen, it makes you want to go home, but we had to regroup. Marcia's grandma was so proud of her that Marcia knew that she had to continue playing."

On the van ride to the rink for the game against Denmark, Jan opened her e-mail and read a letter from a reporter who wanted verification of a story that the Canadian women's team and U.S. men's team were given a warning by officials for swear-ing. There was no truth to it, but it shook up Jan. As Sandra noted, it did not make for a peak performance state, but the team talked and worked it out and beat Denmark.

Later that day Canadian Curling Association general manager Dave Parkes called the team together for a quick meeting to apprise it of the news about Canadian snowboarder Ross Rebagliati. He had tested positive for a banned substance but was appealing the test. The curlers later discovered the banned substance was marijuana and that the incident had become a national crisis back home.

The women won the remainder of their round-robin games, even though Jan had to fight off the effects of the flu and sit out one match. The Canadians faced Great Britain in one semi-final, while Sweden had Denmark in the other. The night before her match, Sandra had a frightening dream that she lost Sara in a hotel room. She called home just to make sure everything was okay, which it was.

While the Olympic Trials were the setting for Sandra's greatest shot, the Olympic semi-finals will be remembered for her greatest near-miss. The game was forced into curling's version of overtime when Great Britain's skip, Kirsty Hay, made a clutch final shot to score a point while facing two Canadian stones.

Canada had last-shot advantage in the 11th end, but Sandra faced two opposing stones situated in different parts of the 12-foot when it came time to deliver her final rock. All Sandra needed to do was draw to the full part of the 8-foot circle, a fairly routine shot made more difficult this time because she could not afford to miss or her team would fail to make it to the final.

Sandra's team noticed the ice had changed from earlier in the week, the result of weather affecting the flow of the air inside. The icemakers constantly monitor the conditions inside and outside the rink because of their impact on the makeup of the ice. In this instance, the ice had become faster.

When Sandra delivered the rock, it appeared to have perfect weight, but it failed to slow down and halfway down the ice Marcia and Joan took their brooms right off the ice. For what seemed like an eternity, the rock continued to move forward without showing any signs of slowing down as it moved into the house. Once it crossed the halfway point of the rings, the opposition could begin sweeping it to try to remove it from the house. The Danish third started sweeping it, hoping to push it past her own stone and steal the win. Just as the rock came perilously close to going too far, it ground to a halt as if controlled by a remote device.

"I didn't know we had won until Jan lifted her head up and said, 'Good shot,'" Marcia said.

Predictably, Sandra started crying. She raised her arms in jubilation, then joined her teammates in a victory hug. Sandra then walked over to Shannon, who kissed her and gently clasped her head in his hands.

Millions of Canadians breathed a sigh of relief, particularly the Schmirler clan, which had gathered at Carol's house to watch the game broadcast live on television in the early-morning hours. Shirley and Art had come from Biggar to drive Sara back to Regina after the tournament, and they witnessed their daughters acting strangely, to say the least.

"At the end of that game, Bev and I were standing there screaming at the TV set, yelling at that rock to stop and Mom's laughing at us," Carol recalled. "Mom's never been here watching us watch a game before."

"Carol and I seemed to have very little confidence in this world champion curler," Beverley added. "We were screaming and yelling and I was hiding under the blankets. Mom and Dad just kind of sat there and watched us go nuts."

In a post-game interview with CBC broadcaster Don Wittman, Sandra said her heart was racing like crazy while her final stone travelled towards the rings with no signs of slowing down. When asked how she planned to relax afterward, Sandra said, "Relax? Yikes. I think I'm melting into a puddle as we speak."

Because it was Valentine's Day, Wittman asked Sandra if she had a special wish for Sara. "Happy Valentine's Day, honey, Mom's going to be back real soon. I love you."

The Canadians faced a familiar opponent in the final. Denmark's Helena Blach-Lavrsen, who had beaten Sweden's Elisabet Gustafson in the other semi-final, had lost to the Schmirler foursome in the semi-finals of the 1997 world championships. Sandra's team knew the great Danish skip preferred an aggressive game with lots of rocks in play instead of the conservative, takeout style played predominantly in the Prairies.

Before the game began, Pat Reid, the Canadian Olympic Association women's team leader, gave Team Schmirler a Japanese good-luck charm. The little memento seemed to work immediately. For the first time in the tournament, the

Canadians won the coin toss that determined last-rock advantage at the start of the game.

The Canadians planned to play conservatively at the outset, waiting for the right opportunity to apply pressure. It took all of one shot for that plan to be obliterated.

Blach-Lavrsen asked her lead to throw her first stone into the rings. It's a conservative strategy to start the game and is usually followed by the opposition hitting it and keeping things clean for the first end. However, the Danish stone came up heavy and sailed through the rings. Essentially it was a wasted shot, although sometimes that happens at the beginning of the game as the players are trying to figure out the ice conditions, while also battling nerves. Sandra responded by asking Marcia to throw up a corner guard tight to the rings, rather than trying to put a rock in the house and hoping the Danes would miss hit. By putting up a tight corner guard, it sets up a shot for later use in case the path to the button becomes cluttered. Paul Savage, the fifth player on the Canadian men's team, couldn't believe Sandra's aggressiveness in the most important game of her life. It was as if she'd been saving that strategic manoeuvre for this important game.

The Danes made several misses in the end, but Blach-Lavrsen appeared to have bailed out her team by drawing to the top of two Canadian stones in the four-foot. Sandra responded by gently tapping back the Danish stone to score three. She celebrated with a clenched fist, knowing that she had made a clutch shot.

The Danes narrowed the gap to 3–2 in the next end but were

down 5–2 at the break. Sandra made a pistol of a shot in the sixth end, executing a dynamite double takeout, which contributed to a miss by the Danes and a steal of one point for Canada. In the seventh end, the Danes scored two, but the Canadians rebounded with a key point in the eighth by promoting one rock with another to the four-foot. If Sandra had missed, the score would have been 6–5 with two ends to play and plenty of time for the Danes to make a move. The Canadians forced the Danish team to score one in the ninth and surrender last-rock advantage in the last end.

Joan McCusker solidified her place as the best women's second in the world by removing three stones with one stone on her second shot — and celebrated by pounding her broom handle like a piston on the ice. In a somewhat anti-climatic ending, Sandra ran the Danes out of rocks with a takeout on her first shot. Canada had won the gold.

After the traditional handshakes with each member of the opposition team, Team Schmirler engaged in a group hug. Then each woman headed for her husband for more teary embraces.

While much of Canada celebrated the victory, which was televised live in its entirety, at least two members of Sandra's family missed the game. Beverley couldn't watch it because she had the flu, and hasn't seen the game to this day. Carol's eldest daughter, Chelsea, also missed the game, although for a completely different reason than her aunt's. Chelsea went to a school dance.

"They announced at the dance that Sandra had won the gold," Carol said. "The boys in the class couldn't believe

Chelsea would go to the school dance instead of watching her aunt win gold. It's kind of a guy thing."

In an interview after the game, Sandra talked about her team's dedication, its hard work, and its ability to deal with pressure, but she also noted that other teams are capable of doing the same. She admitted she didn't know why they were the ones that had been able to bring it all together, but added, "I'm glad it is us because we're living a dream and getting an experience I don't think we'll ever forget."

Watching the game on television back home, Ontario's Anne Merklinger felt the win symbolized the magic of Team Schmirler and, in particular, the skip.

"She was the chosen," Anne said. "She was given this gift. She and her teammates were chosen to have this success."

After the gold-medal game, the *New York Times* printed on its front page a photo of Sandra delivering a stone. Truly, the woman from Biggar hit the big time in the Big Apple.

The Canadian women then prepared for the victory presentation, the closing punctuation of their incredible emotional journey.

"They marched us out and my heart was just racing," Sandra told Sara in her diary. "We took our position behind the podium, then they brought the medals out. And they announced, 'Gold medallist, Canada.' We stepped up and I could feel my body shake. They presented the medals and I started to cry. All our hard work, perseverance and sacrifice had now paid off, a feeling of being on top of the world. I try to keep myself together for the anthem. Jan is really feeling the emotion. I put my arm around her to let her know I'm there for her. Not sure if she even noticed, but it made me feel like a support for her.

"I can hear us all belt out the anthem. What a feeling of pride I feel deep down in my heart. The anthem ends and we wave our flowers and bask in the moment. I see Daddy and I immediately think of you, Sara."

· · · · · ·

As a tribute to Sara following the Olympic win, Sandra's child-hood friend Georgina (Walker) Bergen put Sandra's grade school autobiographical assignment in a decorative binder, and added some articles and thoughts of her own.

Georgina described how her family grew up across the street from the Schmirlers.

"This was an ideal situation for young friendship to develop even though the Schmirler girls and the Walker girls were as different as day and night," she wrote. She added how life's circumstances became "very different" for Sandra and Georgina and how they had grown apart as they grew up. But, Georgina said, she could never forget the fond memories she and Sandra had of their Biggar days.

"Georgina is now grown with five daughters of her own," she wrote to Sara in closing. "When her second daughter was born, she wanted to give her a name of someone who had had positive influences in her [mother's] rather mixed up life. That daughter's name is Sandra."

In another note, Georgina talked about how Sandra had changed her attitude about curling. "Curling to me used to be as interesting as watching paint dry," Georgina wrote. "Over the years, I started watching it a bit while your mom curled. [Seeing her become] Canadian champion and world champion was exciting enough to watch, but nothing compared to the Olympic Trials. I kept telling your mother all the way through the trials to quit doubting herself and eventually she did listen."

Star Quality

Now that the gold medal was safely secured, Team Schmirler could relax. The team made use of the rest of its time at the games by going to the Olympic Village for some of the remaining events and a memorable interview with CBC host Terry Leibel in the broadcast centre at midnight. Sandra recorded her thoughts for Sara.

"This is so cool. This is something you see on TV while the Olympics are going on. Never in our wildest dreams did we ever think this would happen to us. The interview was a lot of fun.

Terry Leibel was great and it was good to see some familiar faces with CBC."

The team proudly showed its medals to the Canadian men's hockey team, made up of many high-profile stars from the National Hockey League. Sandra and Jan encountered superstar Wayne Gretzky sitting by himself in the Athletes Village cafeteria one day. Jan walked over to him and acted as if she didn't know he was the Great One. "And you are? And you play what sport?"

"Of course Jan and I are both trying to be somewhat cool about the whole thing," Sandra wrote in her journal. "It is hard not to freak because these people are so famous. Anyway, [Wayne] is very gracious. We talk about their upcoming games, show them the gold medal, take some pictures. They are pretty impressed with the medal. We begin to realize these are just regular guys who make lots of cash."

When the women returned to Regina, they saw a mass of humanity waiting for them. Family, friends, and fans had flocked to the small local airport to welcome them home. Shannon, who along with the other husbands had arrived home on an earlier flight, was the first to see Sara, who had been brought to the airport by Shirley and Art.

"Sara kind of recognized me," Shannon recalled. "That was the scary thing, too. The young one is beginning to recognize you at that age. We left her for two weeks and the fear was she might not know us when we came back. She was a little standoffish with me for the first 5 or 10 minutes, but eventually she warmed up."

Team Schmirler was escorted to a room to see their families. It was the moment Sandra had been waiting for since she left for the Games — the chance to see Sara again.

"When I walked in you were sleeping in your daddy's arms," she wrote in her journal. "I could hardly wait to get my paws on you. I held you and you woke up. Then we were escorted through the crowd. You didn't cry but you certainly looked confused."

Ten minutes later the team had to address the media, some of which had come for the Scott Tournament of Hearts, scheduled to start a few days later right there in Regina at the Agridome. The victory in the Scott the year before gave Team Schmirler an automatic berth in the 1998 nationals. The organizing committee granted the team some slack by allowing the players to stay at their own homes to be with their families rather than lodging at the players' hotel. According to Robin Wilson, the coordinator of the Scott Tournament of Hearts, the champions showed their class by participating in events all week despite their obvious fatigue.

"They were so classy, just unbelievable," Robin said. "You knew the odds had to be against them. They had come off this incredible high, this peak. They were tired emotionally and physically, but they walked in here and the place was absolutely packed. They were champions throughout the entire week. There was good sportsmanship all the way along. They tirelessly did autographs. You asked and they did it. There was never a balk. They were so available, so approachable."

The champions started off slowly in the tournament, then picked up the pace and made a valiant run at the end. This energized the fans inside the Agridome, the city, and the entire province, which has a passion for its sporting heroes. The champions faced Ontario's Anne Merklinger in the semi-final. Anne's team was still smarting from a loss to Alberta's Cathy Borst in the playoff game in which the winner earned an automatic bye to the final. Now the Ottawa squad faced an even bigger challenge playing the three-time Canadian and three-time world champions and Olympic gold medallists.

"When you let that team get that close, it was rare that they didn't pull through," Anne said. "When they were that close, they were pretty unbeatable."

But the magical run finally ended when the Ontario team won. Although disappointed with the loss, Team Schmirler felt a sense of relief.

"After we won, Sandra and her teammates invited us into her locker room and toasted our team and wished us all the best," Anne said. "For us to be invited into their locker with their families, that was pretty special. That had certainly never happened to us before. I don't think we had ever been into a locker room when the opposing team was in there [during the Scott playoffs]. At spiels there is interaction between teams but not at the Scott. What it showed to us was how incredible their sportsmanship was and their support of the other team and the friendship with our team.

"I think the other thing that not many people appreciate was how difficult it must have been for that team to play in Regina [with their families close by]. I don't think they wanted to spend any more time away from their family. I can't imagine what they went through personally and for Sandra in particular because she had tried so long to have a child.

"I remember sharing some conversations with her during the Trials about her not being really sure she wanted to win because she had to be away from Sara. That was very painful for her."

After losing in the Scott semi-final, Sandra did colour commentary for the Canadian Broadcasting Corporation's telecast of the final. It opened up an opportunity to do it more regularly because CBC's executive curling producer, Joan Mead, had been looking for a replacement for Colleen Jones. Colleen had been having trouble combining motherhood, competitive curling, and working as an on-air personality for CBC's national morning show and the network's curling coverage. Joan took a gamble on Sandra, who had limited broadcast experience.

Shannon said Sandra welcomed the opportunity to do more broadcast work.

"She'd say, 'If I can't play, then I can talk about it,'" he recalled. "That gave her something else to do after curling. It would bring some income into the house without her having to go back to work full-time and she wouldn't be gone all that long. She'd do well at it because she knew the sport. She had a gift to talk and express herself."

Robin Wilson said Joan Mead saw star quality in Sandra, though not everyone supported her viewpoint. But Joan kept working with Sandra, determined to make her into a respected commentator.

"When Sandra first started there was criticism and e-mails and Joanie just stuck by her through all that stuff," Robin said.

"She was adamant that Sandra was going to be a commentator."

Sandra was known as a fiery competitor on the ice, but did not initially display her spirit and personality in her first CBC assignment, the Canadian men's championship, which took place a couple weeks after the women's championship.

"For the first three or four ends she was afraid to say anything — she was a little withdrawn," co-commentator Don Duguid said. "After five ends, we talked off camera and I said, 'Pretend you and I are watching a curling game and have fun. Just be yourself. Make like you're talking to McCusker or to Jan or whomever. Nobody knows more about curling than you, the pitfalls and what you have to be.' After five ends you could really notice the difference in how she picked it up and the way she jumped in. It got to be a real nice friendship."

Change was about to occur for Sandra in her family life as well. She and Shannon decided it was time to try for a second child, and she became pregnant five months later.

"I don't know if we were necessarily emotionally ready for it because of everything that was going on, but biological-clock-wise it was probably going to make sense," Shannon said. "I think we planned this one more than Sara. Sandra's fibroids were growing back. If we were going to have a second child, we had to do it soon."

A Hard Year

The Schmirler team began the 1998–99 season tired from the travels and travails of the year before. They had given up work time and family time to pursue their goal of becoming the best in the world again and winning the Olympics. For the first time in its history, the team made winning money on the cashspiel circuit its goal.

"We were hanging around to try to reap the benefits and not work hard anymore, and that really showed," Joan said.

For one thing, the team didn't practise together as frequently — they were tired and wanted to spend more time with family members — and all four struggled with consistency throughout the fall, but never at the same time. Sandra was pregnant by now and suffering from repeated colds, and she did not want to continue skipping the team.

"She said, 'I am so tired and I'd rather be at home,' and that happened quite a bit that year," Joan said. "It was very hard because the rest of us were trying to help her. All of us had kids and we all knew that emotional pull of wanting to be at home more and yet everybody wanted to continue riding the wave. We wanted to take advantage of opportunities, so she was really torn and became quite unhappy. We were all trying hard to help her regain confidence and regain some of the reasons why she was doing what she was doing."

The team rediscovered its winning ways en route to qualifying for the provincials and advancing to the final against Moose Jaw's Cindy Street, a Regina high school teacher. But once again Sandra found herself in a competitive and emotional quandary, realizing that a win would mean more time away from her family. In addition, she already felt physically exhausted because of the pregnancy. The night before the final, she confessed to Joan that she didn't know whether she really wanted to win.

But the heart of a champion cannot stop beating when the competition begins. Team Schmirler tried its best but lost in an extra end. Although two of the four new provincial champions worked in Regina, the Queen City continued to think of Sandra as its queen, even with her crown taken away.

"It was a hard loss for Sandra," Joan said. "She was really upset over that loss, but a month later she said, 'It would have been really difficult for me to play in Canadians. I'm just too big with the baby and I'm too tired.'"

In April, Sandra travelled to Saint John, New Brunswick, to do colour commentary for CBC's coverage of the world championships. Nova Scotia's Colleen Jones, who had won the Canadian championships in 1982, had turned back time to win her second national title 17 years after her first. She had failed to win a medal at the worlds the first time, a defeat the demanding Canadian curling enthusiasts would not allow her to forget. She faced a tough field in her second try, headed by Sweden's Elisabet Gustafson, bidding for her fourth — and second consecutive — world championship. If Gustafson won, she would surpass Sandra's team in the record books.

The classy Swedish intestinal surgeon showed her mettle with some incredible shots while in the third trimester of her first pregnancy. For Colleen Jones, however, the tournament became yet another hard-luck experience. Her team never developed a rhythm — at one point they even lost a player to injury — and failed to qualify for the playoffs. The sensational Swedes rallied to beat American Patti Lank's foursome 8–5 in the final, playing a patient game.

Elisabet laughed when a reporter asked her if she planned to tease Sandra now that she surpassed the Canadian skip in gold medals at the worlds. "No, never, I have full respect for Sandra and her team," Elisabet said. "They are great curlers."

In many ways the Gustafson team mirrored Team Schmirler. The Swedish foursome had formed in 1990 — although three of the members had been together since the fall of 1984 —

and won its first world title in 1992, a year before Sandra accomplished the same feat. Like Sandra's team, the four players believed in one another, shared the goal of wanting to be the best, and were willing to spend the time and effort needed to make their goal a reality. And, like the Schmirler foursome, the Gustafson team knew how to have fun on the ice.

Following the Swedish win, Sandra talked to a reporter about the effect motherhood would have on Elisabet and her team.

"Your perspective changes and I think that's the most positive thing that can happen. She's going to go home after her little one is born and that little one couldn't care less about how she did. That little one is just going to be glad that Mom is home. That puts perspective on your life and on everything that you're doing in curling and it makes it easier to accept the losses. You want to take those little babies and bring them with you to competitions. It's okay when they are under a year but once they get over that it's tough. You just have to make your choices. You have to sacrifice. In my situation, I think work is going to be the sacrifice. I probably won't be able to work with two little kids and try to curl at the same time."

Sandra also talked about Colleen Jones and the pressure put on her and other Canadian players to succeed at the worlds.

"It's not a cakewalk here and the Canadian public has to realize the Canadian teams that come here have to be at the top of their game. If they're not, it's not going to happen. We've seen it with Colleen's team here this year. They played great at the Scott. They were on top of their game. You have to bring that here to the worlds. They tried as hard as they could to bring that here. It just didn't happen for them.

"I think [the Canadian public] can be forgiving and I think they can be consoling when the time is right. Over the years they've been that way for us when we lost in Calgary trying to go for three Canadian championships in a row. It was tough and there were some people that weren't as forgiving as others, but there are really good curling fans out there who understand and appreciate the effort you're putting out there on the ice. You're not getting paid lots of money to do this and you're putting your heart and soul out there and I think the public appreciates it."

Sandra laughed heartily when asked if Elisabet's victory made her want to get back to the worlds again to match the titles of her Swedish counterpart. "The more people ask me the more I think I want to do it again. Winning it once is unbelievable. To be able to do that multiple times is hard to even comprehend. Four times is such an honour, such an accomplishment, for the [Swedish] team. When I watch anybody win it, it makes me hungry to be back here because it's such a great event to play in."

"The Cancer from Mars"

In the spring of 1999, over a period of only two months, the Schmirler-England family experienced the full cycle of life. In April, Art Schmirler succumbed to cancer of the esophagus at age 64. He had been diagnosed with the disease in 1997; doctors attributed it to smoking. He had his esophagus surgically removed a couple of months after the diagnosis and recuperated to share in his daughter's greatest curling triumph, the gold in the Olympic Games. Then on June 30, Sandra delivered her second daughter, Jenna Shirley.

Because of the fibroid surgery Sandra had undergone to help

conceive the first time, the doctors did not want her to go into labour for fear it would cause a rupture. As with Sara, Sandra had the baby delivered by caesarean section two and a half weeks before full term. Jenna's first name did not have any particular meaning, but she derived her middle name from her maternal grandmother.

Jenna's birth immediately helped relieve the agonizing back pains Sandra had been suffering for several weeks. She had suffered acute neck pains in April when she was driving back to Regina from Biggar. Chiropractic therapy brought some relief. She had similar treatment and physiotherapy at different intervals to help ease the pain. One night she had to be taken to hospital because she was in so much discomfort, thinking it was related to her pregnancy.

Less than a week after Jenna's birth, Sandra's back pains returned, but they were still considered to be pregnancy related. Meanwhile, she was experiencing other niggling physical problems. She had trouble fully digesting food, saying she felt as if it were sitting on a shelf. She had to throw up to relieve the feeling. She visited a doctor, who gave her some antacids, but they didn't work. Then she was sent to have an X-ray of her back, but the pictures did not reveal anything amiss.

In mid-August, Sandra attended a family gathering at Carol's farm, but felt physically uncomfortable the whole time. She did not have the strength to hold Jenna in her arms. On August 26, three days after she returned to Regina, she visited a gastro-intestinal doctor to have her esophagus scoped. She also had a chest X-ray. The gastroscope did not reveal any growth, but the doctors noticed a stomach compression. Later that day, the doctor who had done the X-rays telephoned her and told her she had enlarged lymph nodes. This was the first mention of cancer and it devastated Sandra, who immediately handed the phone to Shannon. The doctor told him that the enlarged lymph node suggested lymphoma or Hodgkin's disease. Shannon was reassured that both diseases respond well to treatment but that a CAT scan would have to be done.

Sandra went for the scan the next day, and the procedure indicated a significant lesion (or enlarged lymph node) around the lower esophagus. An appointment was immediately set up with a surgeon in three days' time.

The next day, Sandra had a fever and diarrhea, which were addressed in an information sheet she had been given following the scan. The sheet recommended going to the hospital for tests. She gave blood and urine samples and had an X-ray, but they all came up negative. While there, Sandra and Shannon asked the attending doctor if he could retrieve the X-ray and CAT scan from the earlier procedures. The doctor explained that the cancerous node was as big as a fist and was sitting right behind Sandra's heart. Furthermore, the doctor said, such cases are given immediate priority to be biopsied within seven days.

Sandra and Shannon started to come to terms with the devastating news and to prepare for the meeting with the surgeon in two days' time. Not only was Sandra attempting to deal with the emotional stress, but her back pains had worsened, making it increasingly difficult to sleep and forcing her to take Tylenol 3 with codeine. She called her family and teammates to tell them she had either Hodgkin's disease or lymphoma but that the doctors considered it very treatable. Sandra's words did little to ease their concern. Bev and Carol were in shock and immediately began searching the Internet for everything they could learn about Hodgkin's disease.

On August 30, Sandra met with the surgeon and was admitted to hospital the following day to have a biopsy done on the lymph node on the left side of her neck. The news of the initial results was not good. Dr. Leith Dewar, who performed the surgery, told Sandra and Shannon the node was malignant. The pathologist could not classify it as lymphoma because of the varying cell structure. It would likely take a week to receive the final test results from cancer laboratories in Saskatoon and Vancouver, where the frozen sample was being sent.

The doctors told Sandra that if the results revealed lymphoma, they would treat it with radiation and chemotherapy. Dr. Dewar ordered a separate bone scan and ultrasound for the following day; the bone scan would determine if the cancer had moved to the back, thus explaining Sandra's pains. The ultrasound would indicate if the liver was enlarged, which is an effect of lymphoma.

The day after the scan and ultrasound, Sandra woke up in the hospital with a fever and swollen legs and feet. She and Shannon were told that the problem appeared not to be lymphoma but might be even more serious: a glandular type of cancer. They were also told that the type of cancer may not have any specific origin, and that the mass may have developed on its own.

"Sandra called it the cancer from Mars because we didn't

know where it came from," Shannon said.

The doctors proposed surgery to remove the tumour. If they found it was surrounding the esophagus, that would also have to be removed.

On September 3, the doctors told Sandra and Shannon that even though all the results had not been received from the pathologist, lymphoma had now definitely been dismissed.

Two days later, Sandra was still in hospital and the swelling in her legs and feet had not subsided despite a drug prescribed the day before. Dr. John Burgess, who was to perform the surgery, visited her and Shannon and said the procedure had to be done ahead of schedule. He said Sandra had an elevated pulse rate, decreased blood pressure, and an alarmingly low oxygen level. He explained the tumour had caused a mechanical problem and the mass had to be removed before it became an emergency surgery situation.

By this time, the media had become aware of Sandra's condition, and her teammates were suddenly besieged with calls. They decided to go to the hospital and sit with Sandra's family while the surgery took place. The day was September 6, a day which became paramount in Sandra's spiritual life.

During the procedure, a dead (or necrotic) piece of the tumour broke off, releasing a blood clot into Sandra's lung. She nearly lost her life on the table. Her heart stopped, requiring emergency massage.

Following the surgery, Sandra recovered in the intensive care unit. In her second day in ICU, Carol and Beverley were alone with her in the room. Sandra began to talk, wondering aloud about another presence in the room, someone who was standing behind her sisters. She said it was their father. Beverley and Carol asked Sandra what their father looked like and what he was doing.

"She didn't really say what he looked like, only 'He's just standing there looking at me,'" Beverley said. "That was all she said. She was in and out [of consciousness] a lot then. Carol and I kind of laughed it off as Sandra being on morphine."

Only in the final days of Sandra's life, when she again talked about the presence of her father in the room, would her two sisters and some other family members and friends believe that Art Schmirler's spirit had been present in the room six months before.

"She wasn't ready to go yet, she had other things to do, that's what I read into it," Beverley said. "What was he doing there that time? When he came the second time, did he come to take her? There had to have been a reason for him being there the first time."

After two days in ICU, Sandra was moved into a regular room. The family issued a news release through the hospital to say that Sandra had been moved out of intensive care after cancer surgery but remained in serious condition. The release acknowledged the family's appreciation of the many calls and letters from well-wishers and made its request for two things: privacy to deal with the seriousness of Sandra's situation and continued prayers. The statement asked the media to leave in peace Sandra's family, friends, teammates, and the medical staff. For people who wanted to make donations, the release listed the Canadian Cancer Society and the Hospitals of Regina Foundation Neo-Natal Intensive Care Unit.

On September 13, Sandra resumed a journal she had started in late August. She talked about what the doctors told her had happened on the operating table.

"Dr. Burgess saved my life that day . . . really makes you reflect on various things . . . how you live your life, what is important. DON'T SWEAT THE SMALL STUFF. Enjoy your kids and family each and every day. What a reality check."

Sandra still had swollen and sore legs and had to sleep hunched over, although she was determined to sleep on her back.

Carol and Beverley organized Sara's second birthday in the hospital, and Sandra wrote of the party in her journal a few days later:

"Sara had fun and was bringing her toys to me to see. Was great to have her do that. She had a great party. 'Party . . . happy . . . mine' were her favourite words. We were going to have Jenna's christening then, but [it was a] good thing I changed my mind as the party wore me out. I still wasn't rested to the point of being normal."

During Sandra's stay in the hospital following surgery, Ontario curler Anne Merklinger developed an idea for a curling lapel pin that would show support for Sandra from competitors on the women's tour. After receiving Sandra's blessing, Anne and her teammates drew up a design that featured a heart in the middle of four arms locked hand-in-hand to symbolize team unity. They created the design on an envelope at the wedding reception of *Ottawa Sun* curling writer Barre Campbell. Anne

sent the design to Regina's Laurie Artiss Ltd., a company spe-
cializing in producing pins for national sports organizations, to
help with the prototype. The Canadian Curling Association
agreed to pay for the pins, and Laurie Artiss agreed to produce
them at cost.

Laurie Artiss's vice-president of marketing, Chris Pasterfield,
suggested producing a separate batch of pins in a different colour
and making them available for anyone to purchase. Sandra
agreed to the selling of the second pin as long as the proceeds
went to the two charities designated by Shannon and her.

In an entry dated September 16, Sandra noted that she had
woken up early after failing to sleep because of restlessness in the
ward. She planned to have a grape drink and open her mail in
the hallway.

"Had a shower and you really appreciate your freedom not to
depend on anyone. To do things on your own is one great gift."

She was released from hospital the following day, while await-
ing the results of the tests done on her before the surgery.

• • • • • •

Sandra started contacting various clinics in North America for
more information about her sickness and possible treatments
and cures. On September 20, she got in touch with Bill O'Neill,
founder of the Canadian Cancer Research Group in Ottawa.
Bill, whose group is not affiliated with the Canadian Cancer
Society, had heard of Sandra's illness and wanted to contact her.
Through a series of contacts, he was able to get a message to Pat
Reid, the longtime associate of the Schmirler foursome. Pat for-

warded the information about the Canadian Cancer Research Group to Sandra.

Sandra was interested in what she read and called Bill, who told her how his organization treats cancer patients with ortho-molecular therapy to build up their immune system. Unlike chemotherapy, which is a composite toxic solution designed to treat a particular cancer, orthomolecular therapy is specifically targeted to an individual's body chemistry. Because the Canadian Cancer Research Group is a private organization, it is not covered by provincial health care. Costs could amount to some $7,500 a year in analysis and treatment.

On September 22, almost a month after diagnosing Sandra with cancer, the doctors finally had a name for her particular case: metastatic adeno carcinoma with an unknown primary site. In laymen's terms, it was a tumour, composed of glandular tissue, that had spread from a site that no longer existed. Hence Sandra's expression, "the cancer from Mars."

The course of chemotherapy treatment doctors were pre-scribing was outlined to Sandra. She would have four separate treatments, each lasting four hours in one day, at three-week intervals. The toxic chemicals would be administered intra-venously and could produce nausea and vomiting, hair loss, soreness in the mouth, diarrhea, and numbness. The hair loss, which occurs because the chemicals attack the follicles, worried Sandra the most.

Because the primary site was not known and thus there was no way to target the cancer, doctors would have to medicate her system and hope it worked. Sandra began chemotherapy on

September 28, the same day she had blood and urine samples sent to the Canadian Cancer Research Group for analysis.

"It was a tough cancer, the prognosis wasn't that good," Shannon said. "After Sandra had gone through the start of chemotherapy, which was absolutely brutal, we thought we had to try some other treatment. She was already starting to realize the chemo was going to knock her for a loop. We felt if we could try something that would get her fighting herself — and that's what this [orthomolecular therapy] does, it builds your immune system back up to its optimal level — we'd do it. We weren't given a lot of confidence that the chemo would work because it was strong and so powerful and made Sandra so weak, so we wanted to look into trying something else."

On October 2, only a few days after her first treatment, Sandra went bike riding and had a good nap and displayed that spirit in her journal.

"I dreamt I was NORMAL!!"

She also commented that she was thankful for her appetite and being able to eat, and for her friends who cared so much and entertained Sara. She also expressed gratitude for the friendship and wisdom of her minister, the Reverend Don Wells; her beautiful girls ("I love them dearly"); and her mother ("for her never-ending care of my children as well as myself"). She was also thankful for her curling friends everywhere and her teammates. Finally, she expressed thanks to God.

During this time, Shirley had decided to sell her home in Biggar and hoped to move to a condominium in Regina to be close to her daughter's home, no matter how Sandra responded to treatment. Having dealt with her husband's cancer, Shirley knew the disease could not be trusted, although everyone in the family assumed Sandra would become healthy again. Shirley and Sandra were making plans for the fun times they would experience together doing "mom and daughter stuff and helping her to raise the baby."

Early in her treatment, Sandra suffered fatigue, nausea, and vomiting, although she felt well enough on October 8 to attend the book launch at the Agridome of *Gold on Ice*. The entire team gathered for the event, but it was made clear to the media that Sandra would not answer any questions about her health. The following day she went to the Agridome for some curling. The day after that she attended a book signing for two hours.

It was around this point that her hair started to fall out — it felt "just like it was dead," according to an entry in her journal. Two days after making this entry, she had her head shaved because of the excessive hair loss. Although she contemplated wearing a wig, she didn't like the look of it and wore a hat instead.

"Losing her hair was very tough [even though] she knew it was going to happen," Shannon said. "It felt like every follicle hurt. She was so cognizant that she didn't have hair and everybody would notice it and she didn't want to go out."

National women's team coach Lindsay Sparkes arrived from Vancouver during this time to participate in a high-performance curling camp in which Sandra was involved. She spent time with Sandra and her teammates, but Sandra refused to be fussed over, which left an impression on Lindsay. Sandra was just trying to live a normal life.

"I knew she had pride, but not the strength and that clenched-teeth determination," Lindsay said.

Sandra had been reading *Chicken Soup for the Surviving Soul*, a book given to her by Jan Betker. The book documented feel-good stories about people who have survived cancer, and it helped motivate and inspire Sandra. She wrote in her journal: "Never give up hope — as long as there is life there is hope. If I died on the table, then I would have lost this second chance to fight. What a great second chance I've been given. I WILL BE BIGGER THAN YOU!! YOU CANNOT DEFEAT ME!!"

She also outlined some future goals: working as an analyst for the Canadian Broadcasting Corporation's telecast of the national junior championships in Moncton, New Brunswick, to be held February 12–13, 2000; taking a holiday in a hot locale; resuming motherhood; and curling again.

The period of October and November proved to be the most painful — physically and emotionally — for Sandra. She could not laugh at anything because nothing seemed funny. She spent many hours grieving for her life, thinking she was going to die. Normally Sandra enjoyed spending time with her teammates, who helped take Sara to activities, but during this period it just took too much out of her and she sometimes would refuse their company.

• • • • • •

In early November, Bill O'Neill of the Canadian Cancer Research Group called Sandra with the analysis of the samples sent to him and to discuss treatment. An appointment was set up for a consultation with him in Ottawa in mid-December. Coincidentally, the same week she talked to him she started to feel good again.

"Great week. Great feeling. Emotions are becoming tough!"

But in mid-November, she started to feel extremely tired and sore and developed a raspy voice that never regained its full strength. She eagerly looked forward to her final chemotherapy treatment at the end of the month.

On the final weekend of November, Sandra and Shannon travelled to Biggar for a family gathering. It was the same weekend of the SaskPower spiel, a major annual tournament in Regina, and many of Sandra's friends from the competitive women's circuit attended the event hoping to see her. Anne Merklinger's team from Ottawa brought a special 10-karat gold replica of the pin it had designed and presented it to Jan Betker to give to Sandra, who treasured the keepsake.

After returning from the reunion in Biggar, Sandra and Shannon started making plans for their journey to Ottawa in mid-December to see Bill O'Neill. When Scott Tournament of Hearts coordinator Robin Wilson heard about the trip, she immediately began plans for Scott Paper Limited to pay for Sandra and Shannon's travel and accommodation expenses. She talked to John MacPherson, Scott's vice-president of consumer marketing, who did not hesitate to underwrite the costs, even though he hadn't been with the curling committee very long. After arriving in Ottawa, Sandra and Shannon dined with Anne Merklinger and Gerry Peckham, a technical director of the Canadian Curling Association.

"We laughed, we cried — it was a night I'll treasure forever," Anne said.

After meeting with Bill O'Neill for about four hours, Shannon and Sandra collected the medication the Canadian Cancer Research Group had developed to build up her immune system. Shannon and Sandra then flew to Vancouver to see a cancer specialist recommended by her doctors in Regina. Lindsay Sparkes met them at the airport and drove them to their hotel.

The following morning Shannon and Sandra met with the oncologist, but didn't learn anything new. In fact, Sandra later called it a waste of time. They spent the rest of the day at Lindsay's condominium, but it became a nightmarish experience. Sandra had been feeling weak and nauseated from all the travelling and retired to Lindsay's bed to sleep. A fire alarm awakened her from her peaceful nap, and she and the others had to walk down eight flights of stairs and outside into the pouring rain. They found refuge in a closed unit and cuddled up in a blanket until the fire department shut off the false alarm and they were able to return to the condominium.

"It haunts me that she had to exert all that energy when she was so ill — because of a faulty wire," Lindsay said.

Lindsay tried to persuade the couple to stay the night, but Sandra desperately wanted to return home. Lindsay understood this longing and appreciated the time she had to spend with Sandra, brief though it was.

Sandra's sickness worsened when she returned home, and on December 27 she entered hospital suffering from pneumonia.

She spent New Year's Eve in the hospital, counting the minutes until midnight, but fell asleep 15 minutes before the start of the new millennium.

11

"This Is My Life"

The new year brought hope for Sandra, who returned home on January 2, and continued radiation treatments, which had begun December 29 and continued to January 11. She experienced trouble swallowing and returned to the hospital from January 14 to 16.

During her hospital stay, seven of Sandra's current and former colleagues — Mike Powell, Bev Kozar, Angela Taylor, Noel Kisch, Darryl Mailander, LeeAnn Berbenchuk, and Phil Harris — proposed an idea to Sandra: they wanted to raise money for the charities designated by Sandra and Shannon by shaving their heads. Fritz Meir, a member at the South East Leisure Centre, heard about the group of seven's plan and asked to be included. He had survived a battle with cancer and Sandra had supported him in his fight. Sandra gave her blessing to the group's proposal and in return the eight people solicited donations from anyone wishing to support the Shave for Sandra cause. The group gathered at the South East Leisure Centre and had their heads shaved, raising some $4,300. Print and electronic media reported the event.

On January 17, Sandra returned home and the following day she was able to swallow food.

"Everything looking OK," she wrote in her journal.

Sandra appeared to have turned the corner after completing her chemotherapy and radiation treatments. She could resume motherhood, picking up Jenna and helping to feed her. She had started physiotherapy and began some light swimming.

Sadly for Sandra, Joan Mead, the senior curling producer at the CBC, died suddenly of a heart attack at 57. Joan had launched Sandra's television career and had become a close friend. She maintained regular contact with Sandra during her illness, constantly assuring her no one would take her television job.

Lawrence Kimber replaced Joan Mead and kept in touch with Sandra, whom he had never met. Her voice had been weakened by the radiation treatments, but things started to improve ever so slightly as she started to regain her strength. The CBC decided to wait until January 21 before making an alternate plan to replace Sandra if she could not attend the Canadian junior championships in Moncton, on February 12 and 13.

Sandra and Lawrence talked on January 17, and displaying the heart of a champion Sandra indicated she felt strong enough to fulfill her broadcast commitment. The following day she spoke to a reporter, who called to verify the rumour she would be going to Moncton. Asked how she felt, Sandra said: "Well, I'm alive." It stunned the reporter, who did not know what to say and had been taken aback by her raspy voice. Sandra indicated she had been through "hell and back."

"Just living is a joy," she said. "I'm feeling okay. I have a long way to go, but I'm feeling a lot better. It's a long battle."

On February 6, five days before leaving for Moncton, Sandra enjoyed a peaceful afternoon at home with Shannon and her children and her mother. A newspaper reporter had come to interview Sandra about her cancer struggle and her recovery. Although she still had a weak voice from treatments and had lost her hair and some 30 pounds — some of which was excess weight from her second pregnancy — Sandra looked great, all things considered.

While talking to the reporter, Sandra relaxed in a comfortable chair in the living room, watching the National Hockey League All-Star game. Sara lay fast asleep on the couch, while Jenna crawled around on the floor. During a break in play, the television camera focused in on Vladimir Konstantinov, the rugged Detroit Red Wings rearguard who had been paralyzed in a car accident a few days after his team won the Stanley Cup in 1997. When Sandra thought about his situation, she considered herself lucky for the quality of life she had.

"I'm going to live and that's the story I'm sticking to. Okay?

Okay?" she said defiantly to the reporter. "Nobody knows what's going to happen to them tomorrow. You don't know what's going to happen to you from minute to minute."

She described how she had started to venture more frequently into public places as she started to feel stronger and had been overwhelmed by public support. Instead of asking about curling as they had in the past, people queried Sandra about her health.

"This is more satisfying for me," she said. "This is my life. It's not sport. It's my life. It was nice when people came up to me and talked about the Olympics, but we're talking [the difference between] night and day as far as importance goes.

"This lets you take stock of what's important. I miss the sport dearly but I'm going to get on the ice this year and I'm going to throw some rocks. It will be just me and Shannon and nobody else will be allowed.

"It's depressing at times, but one of my goals was to go to the Canadian juniors [for CBC] and [cover] the Scott Tournament of Hearts and the Brier and the Worlds. Here I am. I'm being blessed being able to do that, and next year I'll get to play again. My whole team will get to play again.

"There were times when we were playing in the past and I thought, 'Oh, shoot, I've got to curl again.' But I'm going to enjoy every minute of it now the best I can."

Joan McCusker, who had been the team spokesperson during Sandra's illness, contacted Warren Hansen, the Canadian Curling Association director of event management and media relations, to confirm that Sandra planned to attend the junior championships and to relay Sandra's desire to do a single media conference to address her situation; one-on-one interviews would tax her strength. Warren began communicating directly with Sandra to iron out the details. In her final e-mail to him before she left for Moncton, Sandra said: "I'm really looking forward to this. It finally feels like I'm alive again."

Sandra's decision to address the media was important. Aside from the press releases issued by the family in the fall, there had been few details of Sandra's health forthcoming. The media had respected the family's wish for privacy. On occasion, a story surfaced when a reporter would call the Schmirler-England home and Shirley would provide whatever details she could. While helping to look after Sara and Jenna, Shirley became the unofficial media spokesperson.

To try to regain her strength and stamina, Sandra maintained a daily physiotherapy program and started swimming, working her way up to four lengths. Shannon and Sandra decided she was strong enough to make the trip to Moncton alone while he stayed at home to help Shirley with the children.

Sandra had some scheduled tests after her return from Moncton to determine the effects of the treatment, but in the meantime she wanted to start enjoying life again.

But the day before she departed for Moncton, she unexpectedly became upset and emotional. She was sitting at the kitchen table and started banging it with her hand. She suddenly felt as if she could not make the trip. Shirley grabbed her daughter's hand, fearing Sandra would not stop, and began to talk quietly to her in an attempt to build her confidence.

"It was just so important that she get out and be a part of

curling," Shirley said. "This was all she could do. She couldn't throw rocks. Going to a rink was no big deal unless you could throw a rock, and Sandra was too sad to go to the rink, but if she could be a part of this [event], that would be positive."

Shirley succeeded in calming Sandra down and by the end of the day she felt emotionally strong enough to make the trip. The CBC arranged for her to fly first-class to make her as comfortable as possible. Although the network wanted her to do an interview with Peter Mansbridge on Newsworld during a stopover in Toronto, Lawrence Kimber put an immediate stop to it. He feared it would sap her strength and put undue stress on her.

She arrived in Moncton mid-afternoon on February 10 and was greeted at the airport by CBC business manager Nicole Kirouac Luke, who took her to the hotel. Sandra phoned Shannon soon after her arrival, talking to him about the flight and her appetite, but very little about the media conference the following day. They hadn't talked much about it before she left.

Don Duguid met her at the hotel, and they hugged and cried before heading out for dinner with Lawrence Kimber and Mark Lee, the host of CBC's curling coverage. Sandra and Don spent an hour by themselves before the other two arrived, talking about curling in general and her condition.

"It was heartbreaking, but we had a great hour together," Don said.

When Lawrence arrived, Don introduced Sandra and she gave him a hug and a kiss.

"I was really very moved by the warmth and the generosity,"

Lawrence said. "What a wonderful person she was. It's not every time you work with someone that they greet you that way. I think it was the fact we had had three or four telephone conversations. We were kind of protective of her, but she was really a game lady. I said, 'I'm concerned about your well-being and I want you to be healthy.' We tried to baby her as much as possible. At one point she said to a couple of us, 'Would you guys leave me alone? I'm fine, I can take care of myself.'"

When Mark Lee arrived, Sandra gave him a hug, too. He had not talked to her since her diagnosis because the CBC curling staff had been informed that Sandra wanted to be left alone. Mark was taken aback by Sandra's weak appearance and lack of appetite, but noticed his working mate still had two important qualities.

"She had always had a brilliant smile and that was still there, and she still had that off-the-cuff, snappy gift for the gab and smart remarks for everybody," he said. "She was ready to curl and be back on the ice for the broadcast."

Following dinner, Sandra retreated to her own room and spoke to Shannon again. She still said little about the press conference, which was to take place the next day. Shannon had no idea how Sandra planned to deal with being in the spotlight once again or what she was going to say.

About the same time, The Sports Network and CBC Newsworld finalized plans to broadcast the media conference live. TSN had been unsure the previous week because it did not have a crew there. (Unlike the national men's and women's tournaments, which are broadcast from start to finish, the junior events are picked up only for the finals and seen only on CBC.) The CBC had been unsure about televising the conference and originally planned not to show any footage of it during the junior telecast because it was considered inappropriate.

The following morning, Warren Hansen and Jeff Timson, the tournament's media relations coordinator, convened to address details of orchestrating the conference. They had little contact with Sandra and no idea what she planned to say.

A large media gathering assembled for the conference, including many of Sandra's CBC colleagues, who wanted to show their support and hear what she had to say. Tension filled the room because no one knew definitely what would happen or how emotional it would be. Warren Hansen had been concerned about questions that might arise from the media and how Sandra would deal with the queries. Sandra had appeared numerous times in public and had become comfortable speaking, but this far outweighed anything she had experienced before. This wasn't about winning and losing, but about living and almost dying.

Against the backdrop of a banner proclaiming "Greater Moncton Welcomes Back the Queen of Canadian Curling," Sandra prepared to talk to the nation. Shannon and Shirley watched from home, as anxious as everybody to hear Sandra describe what they had seen firsthand but unsure how much she would reveal.

Wearing a black hat and red top and jewellery, some of which she had received or won at various tournaments, Sandra appeared brave and strong and determined as she proceeded to give an update of her life since the previous May when the first symptoms appeared. First, however, she thanked her mother, husband, and their two children for their support. Then she provided background on her fight with cancer.

"I've been battling the disease since May of 1999 [but] I didn't know it. I was in Biggar at the time. [When] I woke up, my back was sore, so Mom gave me a bit of a rub. I drove back to Regina [and] by the time I got back to Regina, I was a mess. My back was going crazy, so of course [if] you've got back problems, you go to the chiropractor — that's what I did — and the back pain went away."

As she continued, she occasionally coughed, showing the effects of the treatments which affected her voice. She also looked up and scanned the room like a professional speaker as she spoke.

"I was pregnant with my daughter Jenna at the time, and the pains started again on June 27. My daughter was born on June 30. Because of the pain, they [delivered] her by C-section about two and a half weeks early and the pain went away, so they attributed it to pregnancy. But about a week later the back pains started again. Then my heart started pounding, and I had trouble swallowing food. It took about a month and a half to diagnose the problem.

"I was finally sent to a specialist. It was an internist who took a scope down my stomach and found compression on my stomach as well as my esophagus. They thought it was cancer. They thought it was a lymphoma or Hodgkin's disease, but they took a biopsy of a lymph node and sent it away to various places to try and find out the type of cancer. They did an X-ray — a CAT scan — and the CAT scan showed a mass, about five centimetres, in my back. It's actually in my thoracic cavity, pushing on my esophagus, pushing on the right atrium [of] my heart and causing all the pain. So then they did the biopsy, that was about the end of August.

"On September 7, I was still in the hospital and my legs were swelling like balloons and they attributed that to blood clots. That's when they did the surgery and the surgery had nothing to do with the cancer. That had to do with removing the blood clots."

Sandra continued without stopping other than to clear her throat or drink some water. As in the moments sitting in the hack before delivering a clutch shot, she looked focused.

"When they told us about the surgery, they thought they were going to have to remove my esophagus because the tumour was encasing my esophagus. When they went in with the surgery, the tumour had released. Some of it had died and they were able to save my esophagus, which I'm thankful for, but it was quite the surgery and Dr. Burgess, I really owe him my life because I just about died on the table that day."

After describing the difficulty of identifying the type of cancer, Sandra went on: "I had four treatments of chemo-therapy. Because they didn't know the type of cancer, they hit me with everything. You name it, they hit me with it. I went in every three weeks. My first treatment was in September and my last treatment was November 30. In between, I had what they call a thoracentesis. My left lung filled with fluid and they had to drain that. I was in the hospital for a few days, but I got out to see my daughter [on] Halloween, which was important.

"Throughout this time, we were also investigating other treatments. We hooked up with a group called the Canadian Cancer Research Group in Ottawa. It's a non-funded treatment that's based on orthomolecular diagnosis and management. It's a compound I take every day to help boost my immune system, so it will work to its optimum so I can fight the cancer myself.

"We also went to Vancouver for a second opinion, which was a total waste of time. In the meantime on that trip, I caught the flu and had the flu for about three weeks and ended up with pneumonia.

"Doesn't this sound fun?"

She said that with her trademark smile, breaking up the tension.

"I was admitted to hospital on December 27. It was a happy millennium watching Peter Mansbridge count down every friggin' time zone and then I fell asleep at 11:45 . . . what a loser."

Once again, Sandra managed to break up the tension. Then she turned serious again.

"I started radiation on December 29 and had 10 treatments. Out of everything, that was by far the worst of all the stuff I went through.

"I thank God I've been out of hospital since January 10 and I haven't been back. Right now I'm dealing with the effects of the surgery still and it's mostly rib pain and side pain and lung capacity and my voice.

"There were three goals I had coming out of this thing, and

the first one was to look after my family. And the second one . . . because I curl so much I've never taken a hot vacation, so I'm going to put my feet in the sand in a warm place."

As Sandra prepared to list the third one, she paused, put a hand to her mouth, closed her eyes, and almost started to cry. For the first time in the speech, Sandra was feeling the emotion of the moment.

"And the last one was to actually be here today, and I thank CBC, I thank Lawrence and Joan Mead. Wherever you are, Joan, I made it."

She looked skyward, her voice trembling.

Sandra quickly regained her composure and fielded questions with poise, dignity, and feisty humour. Asked about the countless messages of support she had received, Sandra looked embarrassed.

"I didn't think I was that good until I started reading all the cards and letters and faxes and e-mails. I'm the lucky one because I've got so much support behind me. It would be difficult to go through something like this without all that support. I feel very blessed to have that support behind me.

"I'm going to throw [some rocks] later in the year. I think I'll go back to the game with a different attitude. I want to play because I love the game and not because I have to win.

"It's incredible to actually be here. A few days ago I was getting a little bit anxious and my mom said, 'You can do it, Sandra,' and she's been a really big support. She just kept saying, 'You can do it, you can do it.' The physio said, 'You can do it,' everybody around me said, 'You can do it.' To actually be here gives me a lot of satisfaction. It's nice to have the juniors look at you and [see you as] an inspiration," she said, answering another question. "I think not just because of the cancer but because of the curling, and the fight that I've have to go through isn't just an inspiration for curlers, it's [for] people across the country."

When asked if she had any message for fellow Canadians starting on the cancer journey she had taken, Sandra paused and seemed uncertain how to respond.

"Oy ya-yoy! . . . Don't give up because they never thought I was going to make it out of that hospital and here I am today. Live life to its fullest. I now know losing a curling game isn't the end of the world. And just keep fighting because if you quit fighting, then you've lost the battle."

When someone asked if she had considered losing to be the end of the world during her halcyon days of curling, Sandra gave a quick and feisty reply: "Oh sure, of course it was."

Then suddenly Sandra's whole visage changed. The effervescent smile returned, along with her spirit and spunk.

"See, I'm doing fine now. Get rid of that emotional stuff and my voice comes back," she said, looking as strong and vibrant as ever. "Yeah, there were times when losing a game was the end of it and I'd mope for days and I still might for days, but then I'll look back on the days that I spent in the hospital. That's what this has really given me — a lot of perspective."

Sandra was asked about the effect her illness had on being a mother. She recounted how until the past month she hadn't been able to lift her younger daughter. "That was one of the hardest things — any mother would be able to tell you that."

As Sandra finished, a group of young Moncton curlers arrived unexpectedly with a banner, similar to the one already posted directly behind her, bearing hundreds of signatures of support. The banner was presented to Sandra after she finished talking to the media.

Among the many people Sandra impressed that day was her husband, whom she had surprised by going into so much detail.

"She covered everything that happened," Shannon said. "She did it with grace. She looked frail and yet she did a great job. She looked great just compared to when she left. I was very proud of her."

Shirley echoed Shannon's thoughts. "I said, 'Where did that come from?' [I was] just in awe and she did it wonderfully. It was a gift for her. It was a gift for the country."

Sandra's teammates had been glued to their televisions, too.

"We all listened to her voice and were all cheering her on to get through it," Marcia Gudereit said.

"My heart was pounding," Jan Bekter added. "I was in tears."

Stefanie Miller, the skip of the Saskatchewan entry in the junior girls' tournament, watched from her hotel room as her idol poured her heart out to the country. Later that day, the bespectacled skip from Saskatoon led her squad to victory in the semi-finals. Sandra's dedication to curling in the winter and her comment about her inability to take a hot vacation had a great impact on Stephanie. "She had done so much for curling and hadn't even taken time out for herself," she said.

Warren Hansen was thrilled with the aplomb with which Sandra handled the conference. He also was hopeful that Sandra's health was going to improve. "I thought maybe she's got a second shot, maybe it wasn't going to be as bad as everybody thought."

Another admirer was Mark Lee, who could not believe how lucidly Sandra had described her ordeal and how well she held together on national television.

"For everybody standing there, this just wasn't a news conference, it was somebody talking about their life," he said. "There was this hope that she was on the rebound. When you heard the details, it was incredible. I had the impression this was the first time she was going to tell the world what had happened to her and she gave it both barrels blazing . . . It was compelling."

• • • • • •

Mark drove Sandra back to the hotel after the media conference and, in a single gesture, she displayed her unwillingness to be babied. When Mark walked over to her side and attempted to open the door, she politely stopped him.

"Don't bother, I'm okay," she said.

Sandra, Mark, and Don Duguid returned later that day to ask the Saskatoon junior girls' foursome questions in preparation for the final the next day.

"You could see these young women were enthralled with her," Mark said. "They were all from small towns just like her.

It wasn't like [talking to] a journalist in an interview situation. It was almost like sitting around someone's living room. It became very warm and familiar."

At the end of the session, Sandra put her hand on Stefanie's shoulder and whispered in her ear.

"Thanks for wearing the pin," she said. It was a reference to the competitor pins, designed by Anne Merklinger

Sandra was too tired to join her CBC colleagues for dinner. She needed all her energy for the most emotional broadcast of her life.

To ensure Sandra's comfort on the ice, the CBC staff had purchased a heating pad for her chair, which was stationed near the ice, and provided hot packs to put in her pockets to keep her hands warm.

About 20 minutes before airtime, as the stands were starting to fill, Sandra and Mark went out to do a rehearsal on one of the grandstand sides. Normally in the national men's and women's tournaments, Sandra and Mark did their segments in the middle of the sheets.

"As we walked out, the whole place just spontaneously stood up," Mark said. "She's so modest she didn't know what to do. She sort of put her head down. I turned to her and said, 'Give them a wave.' She put her hand up and looked up and waved and they got really loud and that was it. She really didn't want to draw attention to herself. She was very modest taking that tribute."

Mark advised her of a change from the normal production schedule of the show because of her situation. Instead of opening with Don Wittman and Don Duguid and then switching to

Mark and Sandra for their segment, the plan called for going directly to Mark and Sandra, then switching to the two Dons.

A commentator area had been set up for Mark and Sandra so they could sit comfortably behind the glass once the game began. The production staff wanted to keep Sandra warm, but she wanted no part of that. In fact, she refused to wear her coat despite Lawrence Kimber's repeated firm but friendly demands. Behind the scenes, Lawrence had told Mark Lee to be prepared to work alone in case Sandra could not make it through the whole broadcast. They needn't have worried. Sandra handled it as coolly as the final of the Olympics.

Throughout the telecast, Mark kept asking Sandra how she felt and whether she wanted to retreat to the work area in the lobby. Sandra said she felt fine. In fact, she seemed to become stronger as the broadcast continued.

The match they were covering was Stefanie's team against Suzanne Gaudet's from P.E.I. As fate would have it, the squad from Saskatchewan won 7–5, and afterward the greatest skip in Saskatchewan women's history walked over to shake hands with the newest provincial winners and their skip. It was like the passing of the torch from the queen to the princess.

Sandra begged off on dinner with her colleagues that night to rest up for the junior boys' final the next day. She joined the CBC crew the next morning, and everyone talked about how well she had done and how great she looked.

"She said she really felt good about it," Lawrence said. "We wanted her to know that if she couldn't do both shows that [was okay], but she said she would do it."

The only change Sandra made was to wear her coat for the second show, but otherwise she looked as comfortable as the day before.

"She was just thrilled about going to Moncton," Lindsay Sparkes said, summing up Sandra's work at the junior championships. "In all my conversations with Sandra — and there weren't that many — she just wanted to have a normal life again. That was a huge statement that 'this is the way things are supposed to be. This is what we had planned and I'm able to carry through with it.' She knew what she wanted to accomplish in her life. True to form, she was still working towards that by going to Moncton. I was cheering for her."

Sandra's flight home the following morning departed at 6:30, but she arrived an hour early with her colleagues and curling officials.

"There she was again, bright as a dollar," Warren Hansen recalled.

The plane touched down in Toronto, where everyone disbanded for different destinations. Sandra's parting words were, "I'll see you in Prince George," a reference to the Scott Tournament of Hearts, beginning six days later in Prince George, British Columbia.

12

The Final Fight

Sandra's four days in Moncton lifted her spirits. She returned home on February 14 — Valentine's Day — feeling well physically, other than being tired from the flight. She was proud of her monumental experience in Moncton and slowly started to go back to a normal routine.

During the week, Sandra appeared in public for a media conference to announce a trust fund set up to help the Schmirler-England family pay for the cost of the orthomolecular therapy. She talked confidently about the program and her prospects for a full recovery, but her optimism faded over the next few days.

A scheduled CAT scan later that week revealed additional spots around the lung, suggesting the disease had spread. Neither Sandra nor Shannon wanted her to go through chemotherapy again because it clearly hadn't worked, so they chose to put their trust in the orthomolecular therapy program.

Sandra's sister Carol and her husband, Mike, had been visiting that week from their home near Calgary. One day while the two sisters were having a coffee at the mall, Carol attempted to cheer Sandra up by talking about God and the reason Sandra hadn't died during the operation.

"I said I didn't believe that she was finished yet, that God had another purpose for her life, otherwise He would have taken her home on the operating table," Carol recalled.

"She said, 'Carol, He wouldn't take me home. I wouldn't have gone home with God.' We talked a little bit more about God, that she wasn't afraid, that she was going to be fine. She was really worried about the girls and Shannon."

Sandra began to develop problems in her vital organs and suffered back pain, so she went to the local hospital's emergency unit. It was February 20, only six days after she had returned from Moncton, and she would never leave the hospital again. Two days into her stay, she underwent pain management that appeared to offer her some relief. She also continued a regular dialogue with Bill O'Neill of the Canadian Cancer Research Group, having decided she no longer wanted to pursue chemotherapy treatment.

Shannon sent word to the CBC indicating Sandra would not be available to work at the Scott Tournament of Hearts, beginning that weekend, but hoped to be well enough for the Labatt Brier, to be held March 4 to 12 in Saskatoon.

Jan Betker, Joan McCusker, and Marcia Gudereit travelled to Prince George for a couple days to do book signings at the start of the Scott tournament and were joined by Lindsay Sparkes, who flew up from Vancouver. They missed Sandra and toasted her in the morning with Bailey's and coffee, a custom of Team Schmirler.

As the days progressed, Sandra's condition worsened and she had to be moved to the Pasqua Hospital palliative care unit, a ward for patients who can no longer care for themselves. When Joan McCusker heard Sandra had been moved to palliative care, she phoned Lindsay Sparkes. Lindsay wanted to fly to Regina to visit Sandra, but Joan told her that Sandra did not want to see any visitors except her family.

After receiving the call from Joan, Lindsay phoned Pat Reid, who had been attending the Scott as coach of the Prince Edward Island team. Lindsay also phoned Robin Wilson, the Scott Tournament of Hearts coordinator. Robin called a meeting later that morning with officials from Scott Paper, the Canadian Curling Association, and the organizing committee to tell them what she knew and to set in motion plans for a tribute if Sandra lost her battle that weekend. But the tournament infrastructure committee did not want the competitors to know about Sandra's transfer to palliative care, concerned the news would upset them.

"You wanted to keep the hope alive because Sandra had the hope herself," Robin said. "I still didn't believe it. Here we were down to the championship weekend and the teams that were in the championship round were all close to Sandra. Anything that imminent with her was going to have a real impact, perhaps on some more than others. We just felt that nothing good could come from that, plus I don't think the family wanted that attention around them right then. I decided it was not something we were going to let out. It wasn't our place to tell. I guess we were all kind of hoping she would make it."

Lawrence Kimber considered several people to fill in for Sandra in the broadcast of the final featuring Ontario's Anne Merklinger and British Columbia's Kelley Law. He thought of Colleen Jones, who had given up her curling commentary work just before the Olympic Trials in November 1997 because of work and family commitments. Colleen was still in Prince George after playing in the Scott as the defending champion, but Lawrence didn't feel it was fair to ask her to resume her commentary duties, even for just that tournament, and opted instead for Robin Wilson. Her credentials were good — she had been a Canadian champion playing for Lindsay Sparkes and knew the competitors — but the CBC executive decided it would be a conflict of interest to hire someone so closely attached to the tournament sponsor. The CBC chose Sherry Anderson, the alternate for Saskatchewan's entry in the Scott and a two-time provincial champion.

"I wanted to do it," Robin said. "I had had my day in the sun — that's not important to me at all — but I didn't want a curler put in that position. I would be temporary. I would be a logical choice to fill in for Sandra and I didn't want Sandra to see herself as being replaced at all. I was flattered to be considered and I really wanted to do it for that reason — that's why I was really upset when it was felt it was a conflict. [Also] I worried for the position it would put Sherry in and I worried about how Sandra would feel, lying in bed watching it."

Despite her condition, Sandra showed her unrelenting love for her sport and her competitors and CBC co-workers with a sequence of examples of courage and heart. A couple of hours before the final began on February 27, she phoned Warren Hansen, the Canadian Curling Association director of event management and media relations, who was finishing the setup of the trophy table at ice level.

"My cell phone rang and it was her," Warren recalled. "I was kind of dumbfounded and I said, 'How are you doing?' and her first response was 'I've got to get this damn intravenous out of my arm so I can get back to life here.'"

Sandra wanted to talk to CBC director Jeff Johnson, but had trouble reaching him on his cell phone, unaware it had been turned off. Warren walked over to the CBC production truck with his phone, but the line kept cutting out. Sandra gave Warren her phone number and asked him to call her once the game started, although she did not indicate why. Meanwhile, Sandra continued frantically trying to call the production staff and finally made contact 10 minutes before the start of the broadcast. At last she was able to speak to Jeff. She said she wished she could be there and gave her best wishes to everybody to have a good show. Jeff immediately contacted the crew on the headset and told them Sandra had just called to wish everyone well. It helped lift their spirits because they had found out that morning that Sandra had been placed in palliative care.

"It was like a real ebb-and-flow kind of emotional morning, knowing what we did about her going into the palliative unit and then having her call like that," Mark Lee said.

Once the game started, Warren called Sandra, who said she had a message she wanted to have read at the closing banquet later that day. Warren passed the phone over to Robin, who continued the conversation. She asked Sandra if she wanted to dictate it to her, but Sandra wanted to write it and send a fax. About an hour later, the hospital staff sent the emotional hand-written message, which Sandra had signed.

"It shows so much how frail she was at the time — obviously it was difficult to write, it's in her own handwriting — and how much she thought about it because she crossed words out," Robin said.

She called Sandra back to discuss the plans for reading it. Robin didn't feel as though she or Lindsay could handle it emotionally, so she and Sandra decided to let TSN curling host Vic Rauter do it.

Following the game, which was won by Kelley Law, Mark Lee signed off with a personal goodbye to Sandra.

"Afterwards I sat down in the hotel and had a beer with Jeff and a few of the other folks. We were all demoralized that she'd been put in palliative care but we were still hoping to see her at the Brier, but deep down there was this sense of dread. It was a tough moment."

About half an hour before the banquet began, Robin sat

down with Vic Rauter to give him the message Sandra had written, and they discussed how to present it. Robin edited the message slightly to preserve the positive without making it too painful and upsetting the players.

"There were a couple of places where she had a different thought first and then replaced it," Robin said. "It shows where her head was at the time. It was really telling and what she was trying to accomplish with the note. To talk about it is not nearly as powerful as to see it."

Vic Rauter, who began as a curling neophyte but embraced the sport passionately and started playing it regularly, took the speech and ad libbed slightly, putting his own calming personality into the delivery.

"I'm still fighting hard and I still hope to make it to the Brier, not playing but talking," Sandra's message began. "For Saskatchewan, I was hoping to be in your green shoes [at the Scott]. But keep things in perspective. There are other things in life besides curling, which I have found. But I hope to be on the curling trail again next year. And I'll see you all in Sudbury [the next Scott site] in 2001. Your curling friend, Sandra."

More than just the competitors had been affected by Sandra's illness, and her words tugged at the emotions of everyone in the room, in particular the people who knew of the change in her condition. Many spectators were weeping.

"Heartfelt as it was, it still made you feel good because as far as she was concerned she was beating this disease," Robin said. "It wasn't going to get her."

Pat Reid, one of the few people who knew the full extent

of Sandra's illness, said she gasped audibly while Vic read the speech.

"I had to put my head down and Lindsay did as well," Pat said. "There were lots of other people in the room who felt Sandra was putting on a brave face, but nonetheless it sounded quite optimistic, although Lindsay and I both knew her situation was grave at that point."

Anne Merklinger said many of the competitors thought Sandra was simply saying she wished she could be there.

"I'm not sure many of us appreciated the finality of it at that point and that was what that message was," Anne said.

A couple of hours later, after the closing banquet ended, Lindsay Sparkes told Anne that Sandra had been moved to palliative care and likely would not be coming out of the hospital.

......

Sandra began making plans for herself and her family. On February 29, two days before she died, Sandra arranged her funeral with the help of her family members and her priest, Don Wells. He had prepared her for her confirmation in Biggar, where he had lived for six years, and had baptized her two daughters in Regina. In the last six months of Sandra's life, he became Sandra's spiritual guide, trusted friend, and confidant.

Don Wells ministered at Regina's St. Peter's Anglican Church, which had a small congregation, numbering no more than 40 on any given Sunday. Sandra did her best to attend St. Peter's — although her busy curling schedule did not always make that possible — but it had nothing to do with that partic-

A star is born: Sandra, looking relaxed, at the 1993 world championships in Geneva, Switzerland. Sandra and her teammates received a hero's welcome home after winning this title.

Sandra placing broom for Jan at the 1994 worlds in Obertsdorf, Germany.

Sandra watching her rock at the '94 worlds, where Team Canada captured
its second consecutive global title — a first in Canadian curling.

Three-time champions: Team Canada poses with the world championship
trophy after winning the 1997 worlds in Berne, Switzerland.

Schmirler the Hurler: Jan Betker, with a pregnant Sandra — who is looking a little peaked — after the '97 worlds. (Never missing a beat, the press coined this nickname after learning of Sandra's pregnancy.)

Going for the Gold: Team Schmirler in Calgary before leaving for the 1998 Olympic Games in Nagano, Japan. From left: Lindsay Sparkes, Anita Ford, Sandra, Jan Betker, Nancy Greene-Raine, Joan McCusker, and Marcia Gudereit.

Sandra giving sweeping instructions during the Olympics. — PHOTO BY MIKE RIDGEWOOD, COURTESY OF THE CANADIAN CURLING ASSOCIATION

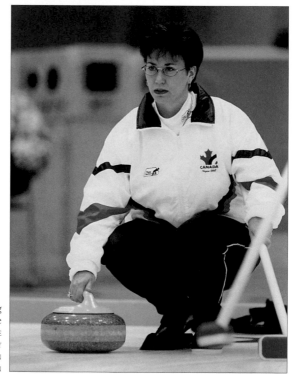

Sandra focusing before delivering the rock. — PHOTO BY MIKE RIDGEWOOD, COURTESY OF THE CANADIAN CURLING ASSOCIATION

Joan, Marcia, and Sandra pose with some curling "fans":
Theoren Fleury and Wayne Gretzky.

Sandra and Atina hug after winning the semi-final game against Great Britain.

The 1998 Winter Olympic Games gold medal winners in curling:
From the left: alternate Atina Ford, lead Marcia Gudereit,
second Joan McCusker, third Jan Betker, and skip Sandra Schmirler.
— PHOTO BY MIKE RIDGEWOOD, COURTESY OF THE CANADIAN CURLING ASSOCIATION

Golden girl: Sandra, holding her gold
medal, poses for her husband.

Back home in Regina at the 1998 Scott
Tournament of Hearts, Sandra poses with
her daughter, Sara, on the ice.

Sandra reading a book to daughter Sara.

Sandra's biggest fans, her girls, Sara and Jenna.

Schmirler the Curler.

ular church: it was Don who attracted her and inspired her. When he preached his sermons to his congregation, Sandra felt as if he talked directly to her. She would often say, "I don't know how you do it, Don, but you always seem to have the right message for me."

One Sunday after the service in the previous spring, Sandra asked him to go into the chapel with her to talk, specifically about her father, Art, who was gravely ill with cancer. He said some prayers with her and followed that up with a visit to her home. Along with Shannon, they said some special prayers for Art before he died.

Sandra had devastated Don when she called him to the hospital in September 1999 to tell him she had cancer. During that turbulent month, when she almost lost her life in surgery and doctors did not know definitively what kind of cancer she had and where it originated, Sandra frightened her spiritual guide with some thoughts about her future. She did not know if she'd survive to the following September.

"She wasn't fooling herself," Don said. "She knew all the time. She was aware that death was there, dying was there, cancer was there, and once in a while it would come in on her and she would say, 'I don't think I'm going to be here in the fall.' We had a wonderful talk that afternoon. I'm a priest and I was speechless. I found the words but I don't know where I found them.

"What I admired about her was she was such a spiritual person. We didn't talk about the weather. We talked deeply about the faith. I told her once — and she couldn't believe it —

'Sandra, you minister to me. I'm the minister, but I come to you and I get ministered by you.' To talk to somebody on that level when they're in that crisis time is beautiful. There's a beauty in that and we were able to do that."

They didn't always have deep, serious talks, though. Sometimes they lightened up the conversation. On one such occasion, he dared to compare curling to bowling and she responded by jokingly calling him a "bugger." Later, while going over her funeral plans, Sandra realized her spiritual mentor would play a pivotal role in the service. It provided another humorous moment that spoke volumes of her relationship with her priest.

"When the subject of a master of ceremonies came up she jokingly said, 'That would be Don, wouldn't it? We're in trouble.'

"She was in hospital with cancer and yet my visit to her was humorous," he said. "I believe you need to take humour into a hospital and not darkness and not death and not hopelessness. Humour is a great healer. We had that kind of relationship."

They also shared a love for swimming. He swam a half mile every day, as he had done for the past 12 years, but sometimes he felt guilty telling Sandra about that while she lay in hospital. But Sandra appreciated hearing about his swimming routine because it gave her the drive to become well enough to do it again.

"Every time I would say I'm going out for a swim, she'd say, 'Don't hesitate telling me about your life out there because I want to do that. I want to be able to get better and go out there and swim. I want to do that.' She always wanted to live."

In Sandra's final days, when she realized she would not have long to live, she talked to Don about the impact her death would have on Sara and Jenna.

"She knew she was going to die," he said. "She didn't know when, but she knew it, and that fact made it hard for her to say, 'I don't mind dying, Don. That's not as much pain as my children not having a mother.' It was a hard time to be with her then."

During the meeting in the hospital room to discuss the service, Don sat by Sandra's side, holding her hand, while Shannon, Shirley, Carol, and Beverley gathered around. Suddenly Sandra began to speak of her father's presence among them.

Shannon has faith, but was "blown away" by the experience. "I think she knew she was going to die, but she said, 'Dad said it's not time yet.' I could see peace was settling in on her by the way she said it."

When Shirley, Shannon, and Don left the room after talking about the service, Sandra's sisters stayed with her. Sandra spoke again about her father's presence in the room, pointing from the window to the couch on which she was sitting. Beverley said Sandra then shook her finger at her father and said, "I know why you're here but I'm not ready to go yet."

Sandra said it laughingly, which amazed her sisters. In that moment, the two sisters became believers in Sandra's vision of her father, believing that she had not had a drug-induced hallucination the previous September when she first talked about her father's presence being in her room.

"It was not until the second time that we realized obviously he really was there the first time," Beverley said. "She wasn't ready to go yet, she had other things she had to do. When he came the second time, he came to take her."

Although marriage and circumstance separated the three sisters, who had not been particularly close growing up, their relationship had strengthened in the past six or seven years. Now, in her last days, the siblings became extremely close.

"It's really sad that it took that illness to bring us together," Beverley said. "It made us realize there were a lot of wasted years, a lot of wasted time. There were all these opportunities that we could have gotten together, but there was always a reason not to. Then Sandra got sick, and all of a sudden you made time. You think everyone's going to be around forever but they're not."

Carol and Beverley tried to ease Sandra's physical pain by massaging her back and legs. She tried to ease their emotional pain by assuring them she would be all right. They marvelled at Sandra's determination to complete a cross-stitch she had bought for Sara after she was born but had never found time to complete. In the final weeks of her life, Sandra worked regularly on the design, which featured little boys and girls, kittens and balloons. On the afternoon of the final day of her life, it took Sandra three hours to do nine stitches of a rosy patch on a little girl's cheek.

"The thread would come out of the needle and Sandra got ticked off, but she wouldn't let Beverley or me help her," Carol said.

Sandra entrusted to Carol the task of finishing the work after she died and made her promise to do a cross-stitch for Jenna.

Sandra also had visits that day from Jan Betker and Joan McCusker, who anxiously wanted to see their teammate and friend. Marcia Gudereit had visited the previous week, before Sandra had been moved, but in the ensuing days Sandra wanted to be surrounded only by family.

"It was just so hard for her," Shannon said. "She just didn't want them to see her like that for whatever reason. I don't know why, though. She never even told me why. I was torn at the very end. I said, 'Sandra, it's so hard on them. You've got to let them come and see you.' I think maybe it was hard for her to say goodbye."

Shannon told Jan and Joan to simply go ahead, and they each went individually — Jan in the afternoon and Joan in the evening. During her visit with Joan, Sandra kept saying, "Don't worry, Joan, this is just a temporary setback. I'll beat this thing."

Sandra's final visit came from Sara, whom Carol brought to the hospital. Sandra had been drifting in and out of sleep, and Sara, who gently rested her head on her mother's arm, looked to her and said: "Mommy, wake up." When she left to go home, Sara gave her mother a soft kiss goodbye.

Shannon spent the night with Sandra, as he had done for the past two weeks, sleeping on the couch. Sandra slept in a reclining chair in the hospital, too afraid to lie in the bed. The memory of her father, a tall, strong man who had become bedridden in the last part of his life because of the effects of cancer, frightened Sandra.

This night, Shannon could not sleep, watching Sandra struggle to breathe in the last hours of her life. At about two in the morning, the attending nurse checked in on Sandra and asked her if the painkillers were working. Sandra responded with a thumbs-up sign.

About an hour later, Sandra's painful journey came to an end.

Shannon called home to tell the family about Sandra's passing. He also called Don Wells and asked him to come to the hospital. Don arrived within the hour and held Sandra's hand and said a prayer of commendation for her soul to be received by the angels in the kingdom of God.

He then spent a half hour alone with Sandra saying some private prayers. At that moment, a pigeon flew to the window ledge, peered into the room, and then flew away.

A Nation Stunned

Almost two years to the day that Canadians celebrated Sandra's triumph in the gold-medal game in the 1998 Olympics, they mourned her tragic passing. To many people, it seemed unbelievably sad — less than a month before, Sandra had appeared on national television and talked so confidently about her future. Now, she was gone, and all of Canada shared in her family's sorrow.

"All Canadians have been touched by the untimely death of Sandra Schmirler," Prime Minister Jean Chrétien said in a media release. "Most of us came to know of her through her exploits as a champion curler and as an exemplary sports ambassador for Canada. But what really set her apart was her bright, engaging personality and her incredible zest for life, qualities that were so clearly in evidence as she fought so valiantly against her illness. She will be sorely missed."

Sandra's death reminded the Saskatchewan curling community of another provincial great, Marj Mitchell, who had skipped her Regina foursome to victory in the 1980 Canadian championship and inaugural world tournament. Three years afer that championship, she died of pancreatic cancer at age 36. The same age as Sandra. Similar to Sandra, she had curled out of the Caledonian Club. About the only difference was that Marj Mitchell had not been married, but aside from that her death and Sandra's were considered eerily alike.

Shannon knew he would have to deal with the media and decided it was best to handle that demanding task sooner rather than later. He provided interviews for the electronic and print media at local, provincial, and national levels. Observers could not believe how strongly he held up at such an emotionally painful time. He asked family friend Bernadette McIntyre — one of the trustees of the fund — to help Sandra and him pay for their medical costs, to assist him with media requests and preparations for the funeral service four days later.

Because of Sandra's prominence and the limited seating available at St. Peter's Anglican Church, the family and Don Wells decided to conduct the service at the Regina Funeral Home, which had a seating capacity of 300 in the sanctuary and room for another 800 in other areas of the building. TSN offered to broadcast the service live in its entirety — and provide the signal to any stations free of charge — if Shannon was agreeable. TSN had scheduled week-long coverage of the Brier, which was set to begin in Saskatoon two days after Sandra's death, and the funeral cut into this programming, but the network's executive producer of events, Rick Chisholm, insisted his company would have broadcast the funeral no matter what it was pre-empting.

"One of our strongest shows at TSN is curling and if you've worked the curling circuit, it's almost like a family circuit," he said. "We have a lot of very close friendships in the curling fraternity and that basically took over in our decision-making."

Shannon agreed to the broadcast with the proviso that the family not be shown at any time during the service. The Canadian Broadcasting Corporation, which annually televises almost all of the national championships, also decided to televise the funeral and partnered with TSN in the production costs. Thus, for the first time in history, a Canadian athlete's funeral would be televised live in its entirety on two major networks. It spoke volumes about the importance of curling as a sporting staple in Canada and recognition of Sandra as an athletic icon — even if she never felt that way.

When Brier officials heard of Sandra's passing, they immediately began going over details — some of them logistical, others emotional — that would affect the tournament. They had to decide whether to scrap the afternoon games that were scheduled to be played at the sold-out Saskatchewan Place at the same time as the funeral. The tournament officials had an executive committee meeting scheduled for noon of that day, by which time Warren Hansen, the director of event management and media relations for the Canadian Curling Association, had been informed that TSN had the go-ahead to televise the funeral. He suggested delaying the afternoon games until after the funeral service and to arrange for it to be seen on a large screen at Saskatchewan Place.

Although some committee members suggested cancelling the afternoon draw, Warren felt that would be a fairly complex thing to do because of television, sponsorship, and ticket-sale commitments. The committee adopted Warren's proposal to keep Saskatchewan Place open for anyone attending the afternoon draw, so they could watch the service beforehand if they desired.

The executive committee also had to address other salient matters: the sponsors' reception that night, the opening banquet the following night, and the opening ceremony the day after that. Sandra's teammates and their spouses had been invited to come to the opening-night banquet as special guests, but there had been some doubt whether they would appear because of Sandra's passing. However, Joan McCusker had called Warren Hansen earlier that day and informed him she and her teammates had decided to come to the tournament after finding out about the tribute for Sandra.

"All of us felt a pull to be part of it — that we should be there — as kind of a tribute to all those people at the Brier that wouldn't be able to come for the funeral," Joan said.

Sandra's passing was acknowledged at the sponsors' reception and the following night at the opening banquet, in which tributes had also been planned for Joyce McKee, a five-time

Canadian champion from Saskatoon, and CBC curling producer Joan Mead. Both had died during the 1999–2000 curling season.

The teams and the rules committee convened to discuss a variety of issues. New Brunswick skip Russ Howard suggested cancelling the afternoon draw, but Warren told him the executive committee had dealt with that issue the previous day. The players decided to show their support for Sandra by wearing the pins designed by Anne Merklinger's team. Many of them had their own connections to Sandra. Rory Golanowski, the lead for the Saskatchewan Brier representative skipped by Bruce Korte of Saskatoon, had grown up in Biggar just down the street from Sandra. He had known her when they were both lifeguards at the local pool. Russ Howard and former teammate Peter Corner, the skip of the Ontario team, remembered Sandra from the world championships in 1993 in Geneva. A few years later Sandra and Russ participated in an instructional video on playing the Free Guard Zone.

Once everything had been worked out with the plans for the funeral and the competition, Bernadette McIntyre sent out a media release. It asked people who were not relatives or close family friends to go to alternative sites to observe the funeral, which would be telecast on TSN and CBC. The satellite sites included Saskatchewan Place, the Caledonian Club, and the Agridome, site of the national women's tournament two years before.

Jan, Joan, and Marcia had been asked to take part in the Brier's opening ceremonies, at which there would be a tribute to

Sandra. The teammates had no idea how emotionally difficult their participation would be. The day before, they had discussed plans with the organizing committee for a procession onto the ice, led by a piper. They did not know the lights would be lowered and a spotlight focused on them as they made their long, slow walk. Just before Joan stepped onto the ice, she developed an overwhelming feeling that something wasn't right.

"I said to the girls, 'Oh my God, this is wrong, we'll never be able to have all four of us walk onto a competing surface again,' and that hurt. That hurt a lot. I felt really empty. I'm sure it was therapeutic to get it over with — the walk onto an ice surface with just the three of us — but it was harsh at that time. I didn't realize how hard it was going to be to do that. I guess if we hadn't done it then, we would have had to face it at some point in the fall and it would have been just as hard then. It was just another sad reality of trying to live without Sandra."

Following the tearful procession, a video tribute to Sandra, accompanied by Sarah McLachlan's anthem "I Will Remember You," was shown on the giant screen high above ice level. Suddenly the tears of sorrow turned to tears of happiness as the three remaining members of Team Schmirler watched snapshots of their skip in all her glory play across the huge screen.

"There were times we could stand there and laugh and enjoy and celebrate her life," Joan said. "The whole Brier experience wasn't all negative, overpowering, or overwhelming. There were parts when we were on the ice that we actually did begin to celebrate her accomplishments." As the three of them left the ice, Canadian Curling Association representative Neil Houston asked them if they would answer some questions from the media. They agreed, but it proved to be a difficult task.

"It was definitely overwhelming," Marcia told the reporters. "We're all going to miss Sandra so much and that was a great way to honour her. This is the first time the three of us have been out in public together since [Sandra's death]."

Inevitably, they were asked if they planned to continue curling. While it seemed like a cold thing to ask, everyone in the curling world wanted to know the answer.

"If Sandra were here and we said we were quitting, she'd be kicking our butts, so we can't quit," Joan responded in a light-hearted remark that would have made Sandra proud. But it was still too early to settle on a fourth member.

While the Brier commenced, albeit with a palpable sadness throughout the building, arrangements for the funeral continued in Regina. Carol and Beverley set up a display of Sandra's memorabilia at the front of the chapel. The collection included photos of Sandra with her family and her teammates, and medals, trophies, and jackets from her various championships. An enlarged framed picture of Sandra, published on the front page of the *Regina Leader-Post* the day she died, occupied the centre of the podium.

The day before the service, Shannon met with funeral director Kevin Gooding, Don Wells, and TSN producer Bruce Perrin and some of his associates to discuss logistics affecting all concerned. Don had never conducted a service of this size, let alone one that would be televised. TSN had never produced a funeral broadcast, although it had picked up simulcast feeds from other networks. The Regina Funeral Home had no experience dealing with the production of a televised service or with the high level of media interest. Combined with handling e-mails, faxes, and phone calls from people all over the world wanting to sign their names in the memorial book, the funeral home was experiencing the most challenging assignment of its seven-year history.

Bruce Perrin and his colleagues had to determine how much the funeral management staff and the minister understood about producing a television show, especially one as unusual as this one.

"They were accommodating and at the same time very protective of the funeral service and the family," Bruce said. "Not that we were trying to intrude, but they were very aware of where we could intrude [and not]. When you're doing a live sports broadcast, you're looking for the emotion. You want to get as close to that emotion as possible. With [something like] this, you second-guess every single shot as you go along. 'Am I telling the story? Am I too much in their face?' You have nothing to draw on. The first thing was to establish where the cameras would go and then sit down with the minister and calm him. They were all worried it was going to be a TV show and not a church service and that meeting was very helpful.

"After the reverend talked to us for about an hour, we understood where he was coming from and what he was trying to do and he understood we weren't trying to make this into a show. We were just another set of eyes and it just happened to be the country's eyes as opposed to one person."

Bruce talked to Shannon, who reiterated his wishes not to

have the family shown on television. Before leaving for Regina, Bruce had met with Keith Pelley, TSN's senior vice-president of programming and production, and TSN executive producer of events, Rick Chisholm. Collectively, they set up the guidelines for the funeral broadcast, but it was left up to Bruce and Rick to execute the plans.

"We agreed the most important thing was to take care of the family's wishes first," Bruce said. "What they wanted superseded anything we were going to do. If we knew or thought that it would be better television if we did it our way, we weren't going to do it."

"In television we tend to take the extra closeup that perhaps we shouldn't," Keith added. "We tend to invade people's private lives that perhaps we shouldn't. We sensationalize things that perhaps are not appropriate, but in this case it wasn't about television; it wasn't about emotion; it wasn't about ratings. It was about what Shannon England and what the CCA and what the curling world wanted to see — and that was a respectful moment or hour for Sandra and a chance to share in the grieving that was going on around the country."

The night before the funeral, Brian McCusker prepared for what will surely be the most important speech of his life. Two days before, Shannon had asked Brian, a longtime friend of Sandra's and the husband of Joan McCusker, to deliver the eulogy. Shannon knew that Brian would do a good job because he had a good sense of humour and was a good speaker. Moreover, Shannon thought Brian would be able to deliver the speech without coming emotionally undone.

"I thought that Sandra always respected my opinion a lot about curling — and Joan told me this, too," Brian said. "A lot of times after games Sandra would ask questions about what I thought about certain strategies. I thought where curling was concerned, she had a lot of respect for me."

Brian was honoured to be asked, though he had barely seen Sandra in the last few months of her life. He had visited her in hospital only a couple of times after her diagnosis, sensing she just wanted to be surrounded by her family and close friends.

Brian initially thought about talking to as many people as possible for the eulogy, but then realized he didn't have time. He started putting some thoughts together and a few hours later he had completed his speech.

The night before the funeral, Brian read the eulogy to a group including his wife; Jan and her husband Frank; Marcia and her husband Kerry; and Lindsay Sparkes, who had flown in from Vancouver for the funeral. They identified the parts they didn't like because they sounded corny or didn't make sense and added some other things. After Jan and Marcia and their spouses left, Brian read the speech again to Joan and Lindsay, and they provided him with some more material. Joan tried to bring out the things she thought were the most important to Sandra, so Brian overhauled the speech.

"I wasn't nervous about doing it, I was nervous about getting emotional and breaking down," Brian said. "Any time I've been to a funeral, I always thought I couldn't deliver the eulogy because I would start crying for sure. I cry really easily. I had asked Shannon, 'What do you want me to put in the eulogy?'

and he said, 'It's totally up to you — the only thing I request is that you make me laugh.' I asked him, 'Do you want me to run it by you?' and he said again, 'No, I don't want to see it. Surprise me and make me laugh.' I figured, okay, I will."

14

Celebration for a Queen

On Monday, March 6, three days into the Brier tournament in Saskatoon, Canada took time out to pay tribute to the Queen of Curling at her funeral in Regina. It may have been a memorial service, but it was really a celebration of life — because that's what Sandra symbolized.

An overall crowd of 900, only 200 less than capacity, came to the Regina Funeral Home for the service. Thousands more watched the television feed at Saskatchewan Place, the Agridome, and the Caledonian Club, while hundreds of thousands from coast to coast watched on national television. Sandra's popularity went beyond the sport. Everyone, from curling fans to the general public that had watched Sandra pour out her heart and soul on national television a month before, tuned in to the historic broadcast. It would, in some ways, parallel the funeral of hockey great Maurice (Rocket) Richard in Montreal almost three months later.

Sandra's funeral had a surreal feel to it, as technology brought together the excitement of a sporting event and the grief of personal loss. A giant production truck, owned by a subsidiary company of The Sports Network, stood parked on the grounds of the funeral home. Beginning at 5:30 on the morning of the funeral, TSN technicians started running cable lines from the truck to the building and doing sound checks. Songs by Sarah McLachlan played for several hours before the service. Both Shannon and Sandra liked her music.

As people entered the funeral home, they were assigned specific areas to sit in. One side of the glass-enclosed sanctuary had been reserved for family and relatives, while the other had been designated for various groups or individuals: Team Schmirler, the Canadian Curling Association (some of whose members flew in from Saskatoon on a chartered aircraft), the Saskatchewan Curling Association, political dignitaries such as Saskatchewan premier Roy Romanow and Regina mayor Doug Archer, legendary Saskatoon sports entrepreneur Wild Bill Hunter (who had successfully battled cancer), and TSN officials.

The area behind the glass had been reserved for Sandra's Canadian Broadcasting Corporation colleagues such as Don

Duguid and Don Wittman, former teammates such as Kathy Fahlman and Laurie Secord-Humble, and the media. Visitation rooms equipped with monitors seated the overflow from the area behind the glass.

Residents of Biggar, such as Mel Tryhuba, who had coached Sandra in high school and played mixed curling with her, and her longtime friend Anita Silvernagle, had their own seating area in one of the visitation rooms. Collectively, the crowd combined Sandra's past and present, all united by their love and admiration for her and her family.

After the immediate family and relatives took their seats, the order of service began with a collection of prayers and hymns, including one read by Sandra's cousin Corry Day. The St. Peter's Anglican Church Choir sang the anthem "On Eagle's Wings," and Sandra's sisters each read a passage from the Old Testament. Then it was time for Brian McCusker's eulogy.

"I am honoured that Sandra's family has asked me to speak today. I became a friend of Sandra's about 13 years ago, but like many of you here today, I have also been an admirer and a fan. In the last few days, I have heard many tell me, 'I never met Sandra and yet when I heard the news, I felt like I had lost one of my best friends.'

"The fact that so many are here today to remember Sandra shows how many considered her to be a friend. Now, I'm sure that if Sandra is watching me here today, she is saying: 'C'mon, McCusker, let's get this over with! Don't ya know the Brier is on this week? And there's a game on TV this afternoon — Quebec's playing Kevin Martin and Korte's playing Corner and I don't want to miss the first rock, so let's get this thing wrapped up early and go watch the games, okay?'

"So, Sandra, I'll try to be brief, but there are a few things I want to tell people."

Brian then recounted a bit of Sandra's history — where she was born, what her family was like, how not only her close family but her aunts and uncles, cousins, and nieces and nephews were important to her. He recalled one time when Sandra threw a rubber ball and hit Bev in the head. Bev, who was as stubborn as Sandra, refused to admit that it hurt, so Sandra kept bouncing the ball off her head — over and over and over for an hour.

"Through her school years in Biggar, Sandra excelled at every sport she tried, especially in swimming, volleyball, and curling. Although she moved to Saskatoon for university and later to Regina, Sandra never forgot that she was from Biggar and never got tired of telling people she was from Biggar. She was very proud of her home town and her small-town Saskatchewan upbringing."

Brian covered Sandra's life after she left Biggar — her time at university and her jobs — and then he moved on to Sandra, the person.

"When I asked Sandra's family and friends what they will remember most about her, the first word that comes up is compassion. Sandra was always more concerned with the problems of others, not her own. She was the first to show joy at the successes of others, the first to cry when hearing of other's misfortunes. Her curling teammates all had babies while Sandra, who wanted children so badly, struggled to conceive a child. Yet when her friends showed off their new babies in the hospital, no one was more happy for them than Sandra.

"Right until her last day, her friends and relatives tell me that when they visited Sandra in hospital, she would always ask first about problems in their lives. The image many had of Sandra was of a very glamorous person, leading a very glamorous life, but she was scatterbrained. She forgot things everywhere. She was totally disorganized. She had to have jokes explained to her. Her teammates called her 'ditzy.' She enjoyed wearing baggy sweatshirts and sweatpants. To her closest friends, she was the antithesis of the glamorous person many envisioned, yet Sandra was totally comfortable with this ordinary person image. She was happy being herself.

"When we think of Sandra Schmirler, we are filled with admiration for all that she has accomplished in life and in sports, how she set goals and then achieved them all. Things seemed so easy for her. She was one of those people who seemingly couldn't fail at anything, but like all of us nothing came easily to Sandra. She was faced with obstacles in every facet of her life. Sandra's greatest successes have come on the curling ice. I don't have to recount her accomplishments — we have all watched and read about them — but like any champion, Sandra had to suffer the disappointment of many tough losses before experiencing the joy of winning championships.

"When Sandra began forming a new team in 1990, she started out on the greatest curling challenge she had ever faced.

She chose a lead, Marcia Gudereit, who had never curled on a competitive team before. She chose a second, Joan McCusker, who just loved sweeping. When Joan swept a draw shot, the only thing that would make her stop was her head hitting the scoreboard. And she chose a third, Jan Betker, whose competitive spirit once led to her use of language that was a little too strong for the TV microphones.

"And yet, even with these three, Sandra won three world championships and a gold medal. We can only imagine what she could have accomplished with a decent team to support her!"

That comment elicited a huge laugh from the audience.

"Sandra made that team work by making it a team. One of the most common themes I have heard in these last few days — as I hear all the tributes to Sandra on radio and TV from well-known curlers and curling commentators — is the reference to her team and how close they were and how it was impossible to separate the image of Sandra from the image of that team.

"Part of that was just luck — they were four women who got along very well, had similar backgrounds and similarly strange senses of humour. But they worked at making it a team, too. And no one made more of an effort than Sandra.

"In curling, the skip gets almost all the attention — that's a fact that will never change — but Sandra wasn't a skip until she formed that team. She had always played other positions. She knew the importance of the other players and how it can be frustrating for the others to be excluded from the limelight, so Sandra consciously deflected much of that attention. She made sure the other three did interviews, got speaking engage-

Shannon and Sandra, just after they met, at the Saskatchewan Sports Hall of Fame, October 1993.

Shannon and Sandra's wedding day, June 22, 1996. Shannon's father, Les England, is standing on the left.
— COURTESY OF DESIGNER PHOTO-GRAPHICS INC.

Sandra and Shannon, with Art and Shirley,
on their wedding day. — COURTESY OF DESIGNER PHOTOGRAPHICS INC.

Sandra at home with her sisters, Bev and Carol, in 1998.

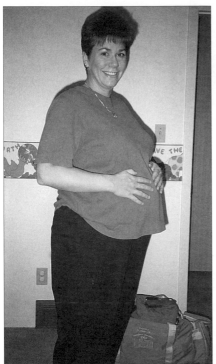

Her best delivery: Sandra getting ready to leave for the hospital to give birth to Sara, September 15, 1997.

Sara and Sandra enjoy a day in the sun.

Sandra holding her new daughter, Jenna, who was born on June 30, 1999.

The team poses for a picture after receiving honorary doctorates of law from the University of Regina in May 1998. Left to right: Joan, Jan, Marcia, Sandra, Atina, and Anita.

Sandra and Shannon.

Sandra on the day of Jenna's baptism. She had just undergone the surgery that nearly took her life.

Jenna's baptism photo. Back row: Shirley, Carol, Beverley, and Les England (Shannon's Dad). Front: Sandra, Shannon, Jenna, Sara, Curt England (Shannon's brother), Judy England (Shannon's step-mother), Sandra England (Shannon's sister-in-law), and the Reverend Don Wells.

Remembering Sandra: Members of Sandra's curling team watch a memorial to her at the opening ceremonies of the Labatt Brier in Saskatoon, Saturday, March 4, 2000. — CP PICTURE ARCHIVE (ADRIAN WYLD)

Sandra's little angels, June 2000.

PHOTO BY MIKE RIDGEWOOD, COURTESY OF THE CANADIAN CURLING ASSOCIATION

CP PICTURE ARCHIVE (CHUCK STOODY)

The best ever.

ments, got invited to the celebrity golf tournaments and to other charity events.

"In post-game interviews, she would always give credit to her teammates. One of my favourite Sandra quotes came following her return to Regina after the 1998 Olympics. She stood at the microphone and said, 'I'd like to thank my team members. Without them, I'd be in a pile of poop most ends.'

"And in an era where competitive curling teams seem to break up and form new combinations on a yearly basis, that team stuck together through everything. If Sandra had not met this terrible foe called cancer, I'm sure those four would have still been playing together 50 years from now, well into their 80s and still making each other laugh at those bizarre jokes that no one outside their team could possibly understand.

"Sandra's second obstacle came in affairs of the heart. All of us have experienced times when we doubt that we will ever find that perfect person with which to spend the rest of our lives. Sandra was one of the lucky ones — she found that person, her husband, Shannon.

"Sandra liked Shannon immediately because he fit the five Cs she was looking for: he was cute, he was calm, he curled, he cooked, and he cleaned. That was all she needed!

"What many don't know is that Shannon is a very good competitive curler himself, but it never bothered him to be in the background, to put his own curling dreams on the back burner to support Sandra.

"Sandra and Shannon threw a lot of practice rocks together. They would always end their practice with some sort of competition, like a draw to the button. The loser would cook dinner. I guess that may explain why Shannon became such a good cook.

"The image many have of Shannon is the husband sitting in the stands, holding the baby. Shannon loved that role. He is very proud of Sandra's accomplishments.

"Shannon, I hope you find strength in the knowledge that you have so many friends who will be there to help you.

"The most important obstacle Sandra overcame in life was the birth of her children, Sara and Jenna. Shannon and Sandra had difficulty in conceiving the child they wanted so much, but Sandra was determined to beat this challenge as well. She had an operation to improve her chances of conception and when Sara was born, it truly was the miracle of life for Shannon and Sandra. Jenna followed last year and was much of Sandra's inspiration for her courageous fight these last six months.

"Anyone who saw Sandra with her two daughters knows how much they meant to her. Sandra constantly wrestled with the guilt of being away from her children while she curled. When she played in the Olympic curling trials in Brandon in 1997, she wanted to win so badly, while at the same time fretting over the prospect of being in Japan for two weeks without her new baby, Sara. Prior to the final game, as Sandra struggled with this dilemma, her friend and competitor Anne Merklinger saw her under the stands and wished her luck in the final. Sandra burst into tears, and poor Anne, shocked, said: 'What did I say?' But that just showed how much Sara, and later Jenna, meant to Sandra.

"I have heard often in the last few days how sad it is that Sara and Jenna will grow up never having known their mother. Shortly after Sandra died, Jan, Joan, and Marcia received an e-mail message from Pat Reid, the former president of the Canadian Curling Association and a good friend of Sandra. Pat's message said: 'Sandra did not seek celebrity and I doubt she saw herself as a celebrity but today I find myself profoundly grateful for that recognition. There exists a photo essay of her accomplishments: Sandra in interviews, Sandra in disappointment, Sandra with drive and commitment and resolve, the feisty competitor, the warm and joyful victor, the gracious ambassador for sport. Sara and Jenna will come to know their mother through the magic of video — they will hear her voice, see the magic of her smile, feel the warmth of her personality, see her joy — because she was a celebrity. I have no doubt that Sandra will remain a very vibrant presence at the forefront of the lives of her young daughters and all of you.'

"The last obstacle of Sandra's life was the one she didn't overcome — her fight with cancer — but Sandra fought that battle as hard as she fought every other battle in her life. My wife, Joan, visited Sandra in the hospital the night before she passed away. Sandra kept saying: 'Don't worry, Joan, this is just a temporary setback. I'll beat this thing.' It was like she was saying: 'Don't worry, Joan, we're three down going into the last end but, hey, we've got the hammer and we'll get our three, then we'll steal one in the extra end and we'll win this thing, yet.'

"Sandra tried until the end, but this opponent was just too tough. It was that final fight which elevated Sandra from a role model into a hero. She fought the pain, the uncertainty, the fear, with every ounce of strength she had. The outpouring of support from all over Canada and the world gave her even more strength.

"Last Saturday, in Saskatoon, Joan, Jan, and Marcia participated in a tribute to Sandra at the opening ceremonies of the Brier. Joan told me later that walking out onto the ice, she was overcome with grief — grief about the pain that Sandra had suffered — grief about the young family she leaves behind. But then, after watching some of the video highlights of Sandra's curling career shown on the big screen and seeing Sandra's joy and that great smile of hers, the tears left Joan, Jan, and Marcia's faces and were replaced by smiles. That is when they realized that we should be celebrating the joys and successes of Sandra's life.

"An hour before Sandra died, a nurse at the Pasqua Hospital came in to check on her and asked if the painkillers were working. Sandra looked up, flashed a thumbs-up to the nurse, and smiled.

"So, Sandra, if you're still listening and haven't switched over for that Brier game, I want you to know that it's that positive outlook on life — that thumbs-up attitude — that has touched so many of us. We will remember you as a sister, a daughter, a wife and a mother, and as a great friend. And we will celebrate your life."

In curling parlance, Brian had delivered a "peach" of a speech. He made people cry and laugh, pressing the emotional buttons that perfectly represented Sandra's personality.

Following the affirmation of faith, the service continued with two songs by an ensemble led by Sandra's first cousin Craig Day, who had been asked by Shannon to sing at the funeral. Craig had sung Alabama's "Angels Among Us" at Art Schmirler's funeral and, with a group he had put together, repeated that song at Sandra's funeral, along with an original piece, "Safe in the Arms of the Lord," which he had co-written with Jim Shute. The lyrics had flowed together in less than three hours, a relative snap for Craig, who finds the writing process difficult. The song ended with an emotional chorus:

There's no such thing as perfection
At least we're told that's true
But we have an exception
You were perfectly you
Mother, wife, a champion
You've done us all so proud
Pain is gone
Rest in peace
Safe in the arms of the Lord.

Don Wells followed the songs with his sermon. Unlike Craig, Don had found it painfully hard to write his speech, requiring three or four drafts before the final version satisfied him.

"The prophet Isaiah wrote these words for us today: 'Even youths will faint and be weary and the young will fall exhausted, but those who wait for the Lord shall renew their strength. They shall mount up with wings like eagles. They shall run and not be weary; they shall walk and not faint . . .'

"But Sandra . . . they will need to be in good shape to keep up with you.

"Sandra, this sermon and yes, this celebration service, is for you. And I must say this right from the start to you good people. It's about when we were arranging this celebration service for Sandra a few days ago. Or should I say, when Sandra was arranging this service for Sandra . . .

"Sitting in her room alone early on Thursday morning — and I mean alone because she really wasn't there — I noticed a pigeon alight on the window sill and look in. Apparently that same pigeon has appeared before, as Beverley had told me. Then the pigeon took off for the freedom of the skies and I thought about our Saskatchewan licence plate motto — Land of Living Skies — and imagined Sandra now in a land of living skies of her own, where she is still really living, free as a bird or on angels' wings, free from the trauma of her pain, yet still able to come and be with us and alight on the window sill in our lives.

"I'd like to use a quote from a great spiritual master and Christian monk of the 20th century, Thomas Merton. He said, as he preached a sermon to the birds: 'Esteemed friends, birds of noble lineage. I have no message to you except this, be birds, thus you will be your own sermon to yourselves.'

"People are transparent, he said, and the humanity of God is transparent in people. The more something is its true self, the more it images its creator; the more it becomes a reflection of the divine. I think Sandra Schmirler was like that. She was her own sermon to herself and that is the best kind of sermon there can be.

"Today, we are experiencing a sense of peace and joy, even through our tears, and we are also celebrating the gift of life — life that is never really taken from us, it just happens in another place and at another time. There is a time to be born and a time to die, as the writer of Ecclesiastes wrote.

"Even Jesus of Nazareth lived and died with an assurance that he was in God's hands. Oh, there may have been times when he would wonder why. Why do things happen the way they do? It just isn't fair. But, because of His insight and sensitivity to the kingdom of God's ways, there was an acceptance: a kind of surrender into the mystery of God. Yes, Jesus possessed a vulnerability to God's love.

"I did find one word when I prayed with Sandra many times and that word was peace. And the phrase I used many times with her was, 'The peace of the Lord be with you.' Those words seem to sum up our faith and our prayers.

"So, when Jesus walks into any gathering — for a baptism, wedding, communion, or into a celebration of life that we are now sharing — we need to feel his peace amongst us and to know that the trauma and stress that Sandra went through has now been given over to the peace of the Lord.

"And I hope that peace works for us because this isn't easy, but now I want to be personal for a moment about my feelings for Sandra. We had a friendship that I shall always treasure. We had a friendship that went a long way past parishioner and priest. When I once dared to joke about curling and bowling, she called me a bugger."

One crowd laughed heartily.

"Mostly, I tried to keep a safe distance from her sharp wit, and in any interchange of digs, she always won. I got to match Shannon once in a while, but never Sandra.

"So many intimate moments . . . hilarious moments . . . wonderful moments. I'm the one who is really honoured to be here to celebrate her life, like I was to baptize her children, Sara and Jenna.

"And Shirley, when I was able to share communion with her in her home a couple of months ago, I didn't think that she would be having communion with Jesus in Heaven so soon. My feelings about your daughter go far beyond words.

"Sandra is okay now, at peace now with her dad. And in Sara's eyes, another angel has gone into heaven, but one who is never very far away. Just close your eyes, Sara, and Mommy will be there.

"Mommy will be there . . . Sandra will be there . . . for Shannon, Shirley, Beverley, Carol, Jenna, and, of course, Sara. Never far away from any of us who have been graced enough to know her for her magnificence, mischief and poise, a very special person who has touched our world and our lives.

"There will not be another quite like her. If we should try to imitate her life in any way, we shall be blessed, but she would be the first to tell us that it is for our own uniqueness that God loves us.

"Sandra was one of a kind — and *is* one of a kind — and her courage, class, and convictions deserve accolades that are more than words can tell.

"Thank you, Sandra. Take care. We love you and know that we are loved by you.

"Thanks be to God."

After 44 years as a minister and less than two months shy of his retirement, Don Wells had delivered his signature sermon. Perhaps only his wife, Carol, who had reminded him he would be conducting the largest funeral in Saskatchewan history, could appreciate his anxiety and what he did to lessen the pressure. He focused on a simple service — a service for Sandra — channelling out the cameras and the millions of eyes watching him.

After a celebration of prayers, Sandra's first cousin Tara Lee Day, sister of Corry and Craig, did a meditation reading. However, midway through it, she became overcome with sadness and started crying. Don rose from his seat and put his arm around her to support her through her difficulty. This was the key moment in the funeral service that separated it from a normal sporting event. Instead of zooming in on Tara and keeping the camera frozen until she recovered, TSN's production crew focused only briefly on the moment, then quickly switched to a different shot.

After Tara's heartwrenching reading, the service continued with a hymn, a commendation prayer for Sandra's soul, and meditational music, featuring Sarah McLachlan's "I Will Remember You" along with a video of Sandra's life.

I will remember you
Will you remember me
Don't let your life pass you by
Weep not for the memories.

People watching the service on television or with access to the feed saw the video, while the people gathered in the sanctuary and in the area directly behind listened to the words and recalled Sandra in their own way, remembering her more for how she lived than how she died. In the Regina Funeral Home, throughout Canada, and around the curling world, people were joined together like a gigantic human quilt in their memories of Sandra.

After the service ended, there was a reception with the family, and some people went to the front of the chapel to look at Sandra's memorabilia, while others just sat and reflected on the woman who had brought them all together.

Sitting among the people gathered from Biggar, Sandra's longtime school teammate Anita Silvernagle experienced a soothing sense she had never felt before at a funeral.

"For the tragedy of it all, they did a good job of telling her life and explaining what she was really like," Anita said.

Kathy Fahlman, who had skipped Sandra in her first appearance in the Scott Tournament of Hearts, wrestled with a variety of thoughts and feelings. She thought about how unfair it had all been for Sandra, who had always wanted children, and how she would have given up absolutely everything she had ever won just to spend one more day with Sara and Jenna. And Kathy wondered if everything had happened in Sandra's life for some reason — whatever that might have been.

"She always talked about the curling gods — and we joked about it — but I also believe that in fate sometimes things are just meant to happen, and it was like all this stuff was meant to happen to her," Kathy said.

Lindsay Sparkes, who had coached Team Schmirler at the world championships and Olympics, sat next to Ontario champion Anne Merklinger and Robin Wilson, her longtime friend and one-time teammate and the coordinator of the Scott Tournament of Hearts. The funeral fortified their friendship for one another and their love for Sandra.

"I'm so thankful the three of us were sitting together, and that Robin and I were able to share our friendship and our closeness," Lindsay said. "One of the things I love about curling is the sense of team. I was so thankful I didn't have to sit there alone and I know Robin felt the same way, as did Annie, that we could all hold on to each other."

"We were so overcome with sadness and yet there's a real strength that came out of it," Robin added.

Colleen Jones, who had flown in from Nova Scotia, recalled the woman she had battled so often on the ice. When Colleen won the 1999 national championship, she talked to Sandra on the phone a couple of times before the world tournament to learn about the four-rock rule under which she would be playing for the first time. Sandra had more experience playing that format than any Canadian skip, and she generously prepared Colleen for the possible pitfalls ahead. When Sandra arrived for the worlds midway through the tournament to prepare for her broadcast duties, Colleen had already failed to qualify for the playoffs and had become the cruel target of the media and the demanding Canadian fans. Sandra consoled Colleen, offering her some positive words to ease the pain.

Immediately following the devastating news that Sandra had died, Colleen anchored CBC's national coverage. Thrust into her role as a journalist first and curler second, Colleen quickly mobilized her resources to line up interviews with Shannon England and others close to Sandra.

"It was very difficult to do," Colleen said. "I've never had to talk on air about somebody I knew who had died. It was a position you don't like being in and yet you still find a way to do it. They wanted to talk about her legacy so much. I interviewed Shannon and I got a lot of strength in that. The fact that he seemed to want to talk about Sandra and share some stories about her and celebrate her life made it much easier to do the job."

Colleen came to Sandra's funeral out of respect for the friend and competitor she had just lost and to show her team's support for Sandra's teammates.

"She was such a likable person," Colleen said. "A lot of times in curling you develop rivalries — and she was so competitive — but once the game was over you couldn't help but admire and appreciate her."

Pat Reid, who had developed a friendship with Team Schmirler as one of its associates at the world championships and Olympics, could not attend the funeral. She had been scheduled to leave for Paris that day to represent the Canadian Olympic Association at the International Olympic Committee World Congress on Women In Sports. Although she had developed a close relationship with the Schmirler team and wanted to be in Regina to grieve along with everyone else in the curling community, Pat knew she could give Sandra the ultimate tribute at the IOC Congress by talking about her achievements to the 600 delegates, some of whom knew nothing about curling. Pat's words to the delegates hammered home the spirit of the Olympic champion, even if some of the people didn't know her or her sport.

"Everyone stood and gave her a moment of silence," Pat said. "Many of them knew who she was. There were obviously some who did not, but everyone did know she was an Olympian, that she was Canadian, that she won the first-ever gold medal, that she was 36 and a mother of two young girls. As I was speaking, her funeral was beginning in Regina. The assistant deputy minister of Heritage Canada, Norman Moyer, gave me a hug and thanked me for having done that for Canada. It made me feel better. I felt connected a little bit to it."

· · · · · ·

The Brier resumed an hour after the funeral. The people gathered at the events celebrated the great shots and honoured the teams before and after the games, but you could feel an emptiness that refused to go away.

It particularly bothered Clark Saunders, someone Sandra did not even know personally. He had come from Winnipeg with his girlfriend to watch the Brier and felt something had to be done for the final game in order to pay tribute to Sandra. He was simply one of her many fans, but seeing the TSN tribute to Sandra the night of the funeral stuck with him throughout the tournament.

The night before the final, with the help of the front-desk staff of the Heritage Inn, Clark spent eight hours stitching together a flag with the words, "Thank You Sandra." He attached the flag to a broomstick and waved it throughout the game — dressed in a blue mask and gold lycra body suit with a design of a lightning bolt across the chest. The costume, made by Clark's mother and grandmother, signify that he was the Golden Boy from Winnipeg (gold is the city's colour). He told his grandmother to watch for him on television because he would probably wear the costume at some point during the Brier.

"The costume stood out and that made people look at the actual banner," Clark said. "I didn't really know much about her. All I knew was that she was a great curler and a great person."

As fate would have it, the Biggar girls' high-school team won the provincial championships the day before the Brier final. Surely, somewhere in the heavens, Sandra was smiling.

15

Views of Faith

When Pat Reid returned home, she still felt a need to deal with Sandra's death. Because she had been a long way away during the funeral, she did not have anyone close with whom to experience the grieving process.

"My husband gave me the tapes and I went down to the basement by myself. I could have gone into the living room, but I wanted to be by myself. I watched all the news clips and the funeral. It was very helpful for me. It's still unbelievable to me. I cannot believe I'm not going to see her. I know it's happened and I've seen this thing happen before.

"Nearly everyone has had an up-close-and-personal experience with cancer. There's hardly anybody that hasn't been touched by that sort of thing. I know that it's happened and she's gone, but I find it hard to accept and I'm sure everyone else does as well. We can't rationalize things sometimes and you can't intellectualize yourself through this. You have to have some faith in something higher and bigger than all of us, I guess."

Almost six weeks after Sandra's death, Shirley Schmirler and her daughter Beverley experienced separate spiritual visions in the middle of the night. It was as if each one of them had been given beautiful and wonderful words to help them understand that Sandra had reached a peacefulness in relinquishing her life and to spread that message of internal bliss to others. These are their views of life and God and Sandra's final journey:

Shirley

All God wants from us is us — he wants you and me to spend our eternal life with him. That's my faith and everything else we do along that walk is filler for our life. If we can touch someone or change something or do something in that life that makes a difference, all the better.

When Sandra was diagnosed, she wept buckets for her life. She had a wonderful life, full of everything you could possibly imagine — two beautiful children — and she wanted her life back so badly. From the time she was diagnosed until the time she died was almost exactly six months. There were six months of struggling with the disease — and you don't battle the disease with courage, you fight for your life with courage.

People talk about battling disease with courage and they're terrified, absolutely terrified of that disease and what it can do. She witnessed that because her dad died in April, four months before doctors diagnosed her with cancer. She witnessed things that were pretty devastating — fortunately, her walk was different, for which I'm very grateful.

There were days when her pain was under control and we would go shopping or for coffee or take Sara to the gym, do these little things that would be fun. As soon as the body would let her, she was gone. There was no sitting in that chair with her feet up.

Our minister is such an incredible speaker. Every time we went, she'd say, "No wonder your church is closing, Don, because you talk just to us." [The venerable St. Peter's Anglican Church, one of the oldest churches in Regina, closed June 30, 2000.]

When Sandra had surgery and her heart stopped, she was gone. The Lord could have taken her then, but He chose to give her six months. Two days after Sandra's surgery, she was in intensive care and we had a prayer circle. You could only have two people in intensive care but they allowed us to have more because they didn't think Sandra would live. There were nine of us in the room and Sandra prayed. I was amazed that she would have the ability to do that.

Fall was her very favourite time of the year because curl-ing starts. As she walked through these six months, God gave her the time to manage her life. He gave her the time to let go of her life and to make that final walk that last five days.

Beverley

Sandra had a love of life that was unparalleled in anyone that I had known. Her love of sport and her love of her family was well known to all who knew her or knew of her.

During the last two weeks of her life, we were with her in the hospital and I observed a change. There were no tears. There was only peace and calmness. An acceptance of what was going to happen. As a family we observed an incredible happening. When Sandra was planning her own funeral, the only ones crying were us. Sandra's strength and sense of humour filled the room.

When Sandra died, the outpouring of grief was incredi-ble, but in the end it was grief for our loss and not hers. She was in heaven with God and Dad, who had come to take her. Dad was maybe her guardian angel.

Now I ask myself, what happened between her near death on the operating table and the actual day of her death? Why was she now able to go to heaven when she couldn't have gone before? The simple fact is that you cannot love anything on this earth more than you love your God.

I believe that God gave Sandra the last six months

before her death to prepare. Her physical life was slowly taken away: first the curling and then her children. She watched and came to terms with this loss.

During the last two weeks she realized that death was coming soon. When she saw Sara the night before she died, there were no tears, just calm and peace. Sandra was ready to accept and believe that God was ready to take her to heaven. She was at peace with her lost life. God loved her and she loved Him.

When Sandra went into palliative care, I was with her one morning by myself and she was in incredible pain. She was doubled over on the bed moaning and screaming in pain. The doctor came in and knelt down beside her, trying to calm her down until the painkillers took effect. Despite the incredible pain, Sandra said to the doctor: "Get off your knees. You are going to wreck your knees." She finally got the doctor to sit in a chair, and only then did Sandra worry about her own pain. At that point, the doctor told Sandra the cancer was closing off her lungs and heart and it was just a matter of time. Sandra held my hand and looked at me. She didn't say a word. She just looked into my eyes. It was as if she was trying to tell me, "Now, do you understand I really am going to die?" She didn't cry. She was very calm.

Before Sandra's illness, I was more of a lip-service Christian. I could say I believed in God but I could not just drop my life and give it up. Seeing Sandra with death, seeing the peace that was Sandra in those last few days, made me realize there really was something beyond this life. It's not enough just to say yeah, you believe in God, you believe in Jesus, and you go to church once in a while. There has to be more and I got that from Sandra.

Reflections

In the course of researching this book, I found no shortage of people wanting to share their own recollections of Sandra. Some people talked about her curling ability, others talked about her as a person. Collectively, the pieces fit together to give a composite sketch of her dynamic personality.

Shirley Schmirler
Sandra was someone who pushed everything. She was never, ever satisfied. It had to be better. It had to be stronger. It had to go higher. I guess that's an Olympian, eh?

During her illness she was never satisfied with "If I feel better today, I'll just relax." It was "I feel better today, we'll do something." And that's how she lived all her life.

Jan Betker

I looked up the word friend in the dictionary and found the following: "One attached to another by esteem, respect and affection." It brought tears to my eyes and I thought if I had my own dictionary I would need only a two-word definition: Sandra Schmirler. When I was introduced to my new teammate in 1985, I had no idea the impact she would have on my life; that we would curl together for 15 years and during that time become best friends and soul mates. I had no idea that when we completed the puzzle and added Joan and Marcia we would win one world curling championship, let alone three and an Olympic gold medal. I had no idea how her love and support would help me through tough times. I had no idea how much joy her friendship would bring to my life.

Sandra was as much a part of my life as are my husband, my children, my family. After Sandra died, my son asked me why I was so sad. I said that Sandra had died and gone to heaven. He looked at me and said, "But, Mommy, we didn't want Sandra to die." I agreed that we didn't and explained that was why I was crying. He thought for a moment, gave me a big hug and said, "That's okay, Mommy, you have other friends." That simple statement broke my heart — again.

When life is good, you take friendships like ours for granted. I know that friends like Sandra don't come around very often, and I am so thankful for all the great times we shared. Thanks for the memories, friend.

Robin Wilson
She was on a path that was charted a long time ago. She really was a winner in every sense of the word and the only [battle] she couldn't win was the last one. This kid was programmed to win at everything she did. I have one of them in my own home that's the same way. I always say to my daughter she's like an angel. It scares me sometimes that she's been lent to us. She just brings so much joy to everything she does and she just wins in everything she does — everything in her life — and that's what Sandra was like. It's like she was borrowed and she was here on earth to do something. She was one incredibly talented, incredibly driven, incredibly successful person. Everybody believes she's up there looking down on us now.

Mel Tryhuba
Sandra had the desire to push herself — to give that extra — and because she was so willing to learn the final details to win and go to the next level, she had a desire to be the best and to be successful. You could never predict this person was going to be a three-time world champion and Olympic gold medallist — no one can foresee that — but you could foresee she had the talent to do something like

that. She was motivated. She had the talent, the desire, the patience, the personality. She had all the tools."

Pat Reid

She loved to play. She was a really fierce competitor. She hated to lose. She had that fire in her eyes for the game. You could see that the game was in her gut. It [wasn't just] in her head. She just loved to play. When you would see her on the ice there was no quit in her. She never lost until somebody told her she had to leave the ice and she was on the losing end of the score.

Don Wells

In a spiritual sense I believe she is still very much present and that she has won. Cancer didn't get her. She has won. That kind of a life is not ever beat. Her life is going to go on in her children and the people that she has touched. I've been blessed by Sandra. My ministry has been blessed by Sandra. One of the touching things that has happened in my ministry of 44 years is Sandra. She was more beautiful than her celebrity status. She was a beautiful, spiritual person. She was a physically good-looking girl and a good athlete, but her wholeness was good — not fussy, not phony, not artificial. She would swear when curling. Her whole person was beautiful. I loved Sandra. I felt so good holding her hand in prayer and feeling the grip of her hand on mine. I'm blessed by her.

Lindsay Sparkes
She blossomed into a very self-assured, polished woman.
She was always Sandra — always with a sense of vulnerability to her emotions — but she could carry off anything
that was required of her with such ease and confidence. It
was amazing to see that.

Anne Merklinger
Sandra's passing at that particular time couldn't have had a
greater impact. Her message was pretty clear to many of us
in terms of "Don't lose sight of what's important. This is
just a sport, this is just a game." That message got out to
many people. Her family was more important to her than
anything. Everyone will have a different take on it because
it's been a personal journey for everybody. For some it may
be quite shallow, for others it may be more significant, but
it would be a shame if it wasn't significant because she was
so significant.

Laurie Secord-Humble
I've had so many people in the last two months tell me how
sad it is that she's gone and how she touched everyone in
Canada and around the world, but to me she was just a dear
friend. I knew what she had done in curling and I always
admired that, but I really admired the person she was. We
had a lot of good times and I will really miss that. It's
unbelievable what she did in curling and it will never be

duplicated, but it's sad she never got to do what she really wanted to do — be a wife and a mother. I was talking to her mother and she said curling was just a side until Sandra got to do what she wanted to do. I said, "It was a pretty good side."

The Future

In the weeks and months following Sandra's passing, several things happened to preserve her memory and contribution to curling.

Saskatchewan lawmakers amended legislation to allow Sandra to be invested in the province's Order of Merit. The amendment to the provincial Emblems and Honours Act would enable Saskatchewan residents to be named to the Order of Merit one year after their death.

The Canadian Sports Hall of Fame announced Team

Schmirler as one of its inductees for the fall of 2000. The inductee list included Wayne Gretzky, whom Team Schmirler had met at the 1998 Winter Olympics.

The unity pins designed by Anne Merklinger's team to support the charities approved by Sandra and Shannon continued to sell incredibly well. By the end of May 2000, 32,000 had been sold at $10 apiece, with the proceeds to be split between the Canadian Cancer Society and the Hospitals of Regina Hospital Foundation's Neo-Natal Intensive Care Unit. At the funeral, Shannon wore the special 10-karat gold pin Anne's team had purchased for Sandra the previous fall.

Craig Day signed a distribution deal with Royalty Records to sell his tribute song to Sandra, "Safe in the Arms of the Lord," in record stores across Canada. Four thousand copies sold in the first two weeks of the CD's availability, following a national press release by the record company. The charities outlined by Sandra and Shannon for sales of the pins received all the monies.

In Biggar, work continued on the Sandra Schmirler Olympic Gold Park, which had been conceived the previous year to coincide with the building of a new school. SaskPower, a provincial Crown corporation that had been one of the sponsors of Team Schmirler, donated $75,000 to the park's development.

In Glasgow, Scotland, Sandra was remembered prior to the start of the world curling championships in April 2000. The women's draw included many teams that Team Schmirler had played before, including four-time world champion Elisabet

Gustafson of Sweden and two-time world champion Dordi Nordby of Denmark.

Vancouver's Kelley Law skipped Canada's entry in the worlds. Third in the 1997 Olympic Trials and coached at the time by Team Schmirler's future advisor-associate Lindsay Sparkes, Kelley had always been on the cusp of a major accomplishment. It all happened in the 1999–2000 season when her first-year team won the Canadian and world titles. Kelley's super squad consisted of vice-skip Julie Skinner, a former world junior and Canadian women's champ; second Georgina Wheatcroft, a Canadian and world champion with Pat Sanders' team in 1987; and lead Diane Nelson, a longtime competitive curler. The team's dynamics resembled those of Team Schmirler, with the women's desire to balance marriage and motherhood with competitive curling. With the exception of Diane, who is single, Kelley, Julie, and Georgina had begun families within just the past two years.

Kelley's title in Scotland represented the first for Canada in the worlds since Sandra's victory in 1997. Kelley dedicated the tournament to Sandra before it started and paid tribute to her after the victory.

In what may have been the biggest news of all related to Team Schmirler, Jan, Joan, and Marcia began the search for a new teammate. It took them about a month to begin the process because every time the three members tried to come together to make plans, they found themselves depressed and started crying, still grieving for Sandra. But finally the team assembled a list of prospective players they felt compatible with to play in cash-spiels, in particular the ones that served as qualifying spots for the 2001 Olympic Trials. Even though the team won the 1998 Olympic Games, that did not earn them an immediate berth four years later in the tournament in Salt Lake City. In fact, it didn't even give them an automatic bye into the Trials because the rules committee had not made such a provision.

Because many teams had already assembled their lineups for the 2000–2001 curling season, Jan, Joan, and Marcia did not have an easy task finding a player. Moreover, there had been suggestions in curling circles that because of the immense pressure of having to follow Sandra, the list of interested applicants would not be long.

National coach Lindsay Sparkes, a former Canadian champion who had not played competitively in 10 years, had been considered as a fill-in for Sandra while the team was still hoping she would recover. Lindsay thought long and hard about that role and practised, but did not feel she could help them because of her long layoff. She realized it also required an emotional commitment to skipping with full gusto, something she did not possess, having "turned a corner in her life." She felt she could be more useful as a coach.

"Anybody would be thrilled to be asked and I was very, very honoured to be asked and I just knew they'd be able to get somebody who would fit very nicely with them," Lindsay said.

That somebody became Shannon Kleibrink — the same Shannon Kleibrink who lost to Sandra in the unforgettable final of the 1997 Olympic Trials. The invitation caught her by surprise when Joan called.

"I thought she was the chairperson for a bonspiel I might be in next year," Shannon recalled with a laugh. "She said, 'No, I want to ask you to skip my team.'"

Never did it dawn on Shannon that Sandra's team would search for a skip outside the province of Saskatchewan. Shannon had already committed to a Calgary team for the 2000–2001 provincial playdowns, so she had to consult that squad before joining a new one. But because the new assignment pertained only to the 2000 cashspiel season and did not interfere with provincial playdowns, her Calgary squad gave her the go-ahead.

Shannon jumped at the chance to join the team, regardless of the pressure. To some people it may have seemed like accepting an invitation to replace Mick Jagger as lead singer of the Rolling Stones.

"Somebody has to help those girls go on because I don't want to see them not play — that's their life, they love to curl," Shannon said. "I thought it was a great opportunity to play with them. They've obviously done it all and I don't think their curling career should stop there. I was honoured that they asked me and I never hesitated. I thought I had a great team going into the season already — so I don't want to make that sound like that wasn't a good opportunity for me already — but definitely I think they're the best team in the world."

"When we finally got to the point we could make some calls and Shannon said yes, that was the first time all of us got excited about curling again," Joan said. "The process of asking her wasn't exciting, but once she said yes, then it felt better. It felt a little bit more like closure, that we could start looking forward to curling instead of dreading it."

The addition of Shannon to the team was ironic. Not only had Shannon lost to Sandra in the final of the Olympic Trials, but she also had the same first name as Sandra's widower. Shannon England jokingly said provisions would have to be made between the two Shannons for conversational purposes. He would be Shannon E. and she would be Shannon K.

Shannon Kleibrink had many things in common with Sandra: she was a thirty-something with a husband (Richard) who curled competitively and two young children (Torri, seven, and Kyler, four). She also grew up in small-town Saskatchewan — "I think all good curlers come from Saskatchewan," she said with a laugh — but in this case the place happened to be Pelly. Pelly has a population of some 500, about one-fifth the size of Biggar, but with the proverbial curling rink.

"I'm not sure where Biggar is exactly," Shannon said apologetically. "Pelly is about two hours away from Regina, but the problem is I'm not sure in which direction Biggar is."

Pelly is in the eastern part of Saskatchewan, close to the Manitoba border, while Biggar is in the western part of the province, close to the Alberta border. Never the twain shall meet — except, perhaps, in provincial playdowns.

Shannon grew up as the youngest of three children of Tom and Mabel Getty, both of whom were considered good club curlers. Tony Werenich, the elder brother of two-time Canadian and world champion Ed Werenich, lived in Benito, Manitoba, about 20 miles from Pelly, and recalled playing against Tom Getty in the 1960s. Tom was a "gentle giant" of a man who not only dwarfed Tony but also had considerable years on him. Back then junior players did not have their own program, so they had to play against adults. In those days, small towns such as Benito and Pelly had one big bonspiel a year — the social event of the season — attracting some one hundred teams and lasting a week.

Shannon moved away from Pelly at about the age of eight, but the townspeople never forgot her. She received some congratulatory calls from some hometown people when she joined Team Schmirler. She also received requests from as many as 50 media members. The last time Shannon faced such a barrage came following her loss in the trials. That was the last time curling fans saw Shannon Kleibrink in a major spotlight.

To help prepare for the fall of 2000, the team came together for its annual weekend get-together, this one providing Shannon the opportunity to become acquainted with her new team members and vice versa. Lindsay Sparkes flew in from Vancouver and met Shannon in Calgary, then they took a connecting flight to Regina. The entire team retreated to a cabin to discuss goals, expectations, commitment, and Sandra. The emotions flowed as openly as they did when Sandra, Jan, Joan, and Marcia played together throughout their long relationship. This union, however, reached an even higher emotional level because they were still grieving.

"The girls were free to talk about the difficulty they all had in taking this step," Lindsay said. "Shannon came out with the fact she considered this to be a five-woman squad. We talked about the number of ways Sandra's spirit would always be with that team. That was an undeniable aspect and there's lots of ways Sandra's spirit can help guide the team through the difficult times ahead that every team faces. I think that really comforted the other girls that Shannon was able to accept that and welcome that."

In fact, Shannon suggested wearing a symbol of Sandra on their uniforms, perhaps adopting the pin design created by Anne Merklinger's team.

"Psychology is a big part of every good curling team, but for them it's going to be even more important because they'll be stepping on the ice and not having Sandra there," said Shannon K. "We'll just take it one step at a time and we'll make whatever adjustments we need to.

"We're not looking at it like I'm replacing her, so when the press comes after us and says, 'You didn't do this like Sandra did,' well, I'm not trying to be her. That's our defence against the world."

• • • • • •

In the days that have followed the funeral, Shannon England and Shirley have forged forward, supporting each other emotionally and, more important, nurturing and developing the lives of Sara and Jenna. Shannon and Shirley have not had time to feel sorry for themselves because of how much the two young-sters depend on them. As Shirley said: "I need them as much as they need me."

Shirley lived in her son-in-law's house, while searching for a townhouse near the home and attempting to sell her home in Biggar. Occasionally, the loss of Sandra dawned on Sara and she would remark to her grandmother: "I miss Mommy."

She is not alone.

Acknowledgements

I would like to thank the following people:

Sandra Schmirler, for giving me the inspiration to do this project.

Shannon England and Shirley Schmirler and Sara and Jenna. Sandra's sisters, Carol Kostrosky and Beverley Hanowski.

Jan Betker, Joan McCusker, Marcia Gudereit, Lindsay Sparkes, Shannon Kleibrink, and Brian McCusker, for their various insights.

Pat Reid, for being a phone call away day or night.

Darrell Davis, his wife Eva, and their two sons, Austin and Tanner, for their kindness and hospitality during my two extended stays in Regina. I am indebted to you all, especially Hershey the chocolate Lab.

Don Wells, for his honesty and understanding.

CBC executive Joel Darling and curling producer Lawrence Kimber, for insights and background. CBC publicist Barb Cooper, for providing me with key videotapes.

The two Dons — Don Duguid and Don Wittman — for teaching me a little bit about curling and life.

Mark Lee, for his honesty, humour, and insight.

All the production staff at CBC and TSN, who were involved in this book more than they realize.

The late Joan Mead, whose spirit is alive in this book.

Keith Pelley, for having the idea of broadcasting Sandra's funeral. Bruce Perrin, who produced the funeral with passion and respect.

The Saskatchewan Curling Association, especially Amber Holland, for providing me with names, phone numbers, and statistics. Also Stephanie Miller.

Robin Wilson and Jeff Timson, the irreplaceable media coordinators of the Scott Tournament of Hearts and the Brier, respectively.

Everyone from Biggar who answered my questions, no matter how big or small, in particular Jacqui Moir of the Biggar Museum.

Canadian Curling Association media relations director Warren Hansen, for his help in this book and other projects.

All the folks at *Sweep!* magazine.

Marilyn Bodogh, Eddie Werenich, and Russ Howard, who have all been a big part of my curling education since 1986, and their various teams.

The Curling reporters of Canada, past and present, in particular Con Griwkowsky, Gordie McIntyre, Dave Banks, Kent "Cookie" Gilchrist, Jim Bender, Barre Campbell, Tom Slater, Bob Weeks, Bill Graveland, Reg Curren, Jim "Hollywood" Henderson, Bob "Starvin'" Garvin, Ken Thompson, George Karrys, Steve Zinck, Paul Thomas, and Dave Maclean; and the distaff side — Donna Spencer, Lisa Bowes, Sheri Hargrave, and Ardith Stephanson.

Jim "Shaky" Hunt, who joined me on my first curling assignment and is one of my idols because of his storytelling and love of life. George "the Baron" Gross, who gave me my first curling assignment in 1986. *Toronto Sun* sports editor Scott Morrison, who allowed me to go

ACKNOWLEDGEMENTS

to Regina to interview Sandra and helped make this project possible. My buddies at the *Sun* — Frank Zicarelli, Steve Buffery, Mike Zeisberger, Tony Maraschiello, and Steve Simmons. *Toronto Sun* sports secretary Sheila Chidley, who is to the department what Reggie Jackson was to the New York Yankees. The *Sun*'s outstanding library staff — easily the best researchers of any paper, anywhere, anytime — most notably Jillian Goddard.

My agent Arnold Gosewich. Stoddart managing editor Don Bastian; his assistant, Siobhan Blessing; and copy editor Wendy Thomas.

My parents Myrna and Lou Lefko and my brother Elliott. My in-laws Louise and Don Lloyd.

Two special people: George and Nina Williams.

The neighbourhood gang: John and Sheila Kennedy, Tristan and Sonya Carey, Marc and Debbie Tannenbaum, Morris and Suzie Tambor, Doug and Sonya Grant, and Al and Luda Abreu. You guys have all been part of this.

Max and Helen Zeller and everyone at Muskoka House. I miss you all. The town of Baysville, the Biggar in my heart.

My wife, Jane — my best friend, my editor, and the distinguished vice-skip of Team Lefko. Our two children, Ben and Shayna, the fabulous front end of the team. Our dog, Bandit, the alternate of the team, and Hammy the hamster.

Two special English teachers — Nathan Shuster and Sharon Holesh — who fostered my passion for writing and love of words.

And S.E. Hinton, author of *The Outsiders*. Stay Gold!

And lastly, all cancer patients and their families and friends. You are the champions in my thoughts and prayers for fighting the cruellest opponent of all. I wish the best for all of you.

197

Index

Canadian Broadcasting Corporation
(CBC), 64, 81, 82, 85–86, 89
Newsworld, 114, 115, 116
Sandra's broadcast, February 2000,
115–26, 154
Sandra's cancer and, 104, 110,
114, 128, 130
Sandra's funeral and, 143, 145, 154
Canadian Cancer Research Group,
100–101, 102, 104, 119, 128
Canadian Cancer Society, 99, 186
Canadian Curling Association
(CCA), 35, 37–38, 64, 67, 72,
161
Sandra's cancer and, 100, 105,
112, 129, 131
Sandra's funeral and, 144, 149, 154
Canadian National Railway, 7
Canadian Olympic Association, 35,
69, 74, 171
cancer, 2, 4, 104, 159, 161. See also
journal
biopsy for, 95, 96, 117–18
bone scans for, 96
CAT scans for, 95, 118, 128
diagnosis, 94–97
immune system and, 101, 105,
106, 119
palliative care and, 129, 132, 134
pancreatic, 142
Sandra's broadcast about, 115–26,
154
spreading of, 128
surgery for, 97, 98
symptoms, 94–95, 103, 106
therapy (see therapy)
tumour, 95, 96, 97, 101, 118
X-rays for, 94, 95, 118
"cancer from Mars, the," 96, 101
cashspiels, 19, 25, 45, 87, 189
championships, 54. See also awards;
medals
badminton and volleyball, 15
Canadian, 2, 36, 89, 142 (see also
Scott Tournament of Hearts)
Canadian junior, 2, 20, 104, 110,
112, 116

Canadian mixed, 23
high-school, 20, 172
ladies' league, 15
Olympic, 2, 5, 8, 76–77
Saskatchewan, 4, 17, 25, 27, 29,
34, 55
world (see world championships)
Charette, Agnes, 35
charities, 100, 109–10, 186. See also
curling, pin
Chicken Soup for the Surviving Soul,
104
Chisholm, Rick, 143, 149
Chrétien, Jean, 141
"circus shot," 63
Clews-Strayer, Janet, 39
commercial opportunities, 40, 45.
See also cashspiels; sponsorship
conference, media, 115–26, 154
Corinne (childhood friend), 10–11
Corner, Peter, 145
curling, 12–14. See also bonspiels;
Brier; championships
attitude about, 17, 90–91
Free Guard Zone and, 38, 65, 145
history of, 13
importance of, 143, 155–56
Olympics and (see Olympics, 1998
Winter)
pin, 99–100, 105, 124, 145, 186,
192
rocks, 13–14, 42
skip (see skip)
strategies, 14, 36, 38, 47, 63–65,
74–75, 150
Super League, 20
sweeping, 14, 64–65, 73, 158
at university, 18–20

Daku, Karen, 52
Darte, Marilyn. See Bodogh, Marilyn
Davis, Carol, 18–21
Day, Corry, 155, 167
Day, Craig, 163, 167, 186
Day, Tara Lee, 167
Deachman, Bruce, 3
death and dying, 135–40